Summer's School

Summer's School

LESSONS TAUGHT ALONG A JOURNEY THROUGH
FOSTER CARE, DISABILITY, AND HEALTH CARE
BY THE BRAVEST GIRL I KNOW.

Michael J Hoggatt

Published by

Hoggatt Consulting

www.hoggattconsulting.com

Library of Congress Cataloging-in-Publication Data is on file at the Library of Con-gress, Washington, DC.

Library of Congress Control Number (LCCN): 2020920494

ISBN# 978-0-5787-8158-7 (Print)

ISBN# 978-1-0879-2197-6 (ebook)

Scripture quotations labeled KJV are from the King James Version of the Bible. Public Domain

Scripture quotations labeled MSG are from THE MESSAGE, copyright © 1993, 1994, 1995, 1996, 2000, 2001, 2002 by Eugene H. Peterson. Used by permission of Nav-Press. All rights reserved. Represented by Tyndale House Publishers, Inc.

Scripture quotations labeled NASB are from the New American Standard Bible® (NASB), copyright © 1960, 1962, 1963, 1968, 1971, 1972, 1973, 1975, 1977, 1995 by The Lockman Foundation. Used by permission. www.Lockman.org

Scripture quotations labeled NIV are from the Holy Bible, New International Ver-sion®. NIV®. Copyright © 1973, 1978, 1984, 2011 by Biblica, Inc.™ Used by permis-sion of Zondervan. All rights reserved worldwide. www.zondervan.com. The "NIV" and "New International Version" are trademarks registered in the United States Patent and Trademark Office by Biblica, Inc.™

All Photographs are property of Rachel Wright Photography © 2018 (www.rachwrightphoto.com)

Interior Design courtesy of BookDesignTemplates.com © 2018 All rights reserved.

Cover Design courtesy of Kenny Nnoli © 2020 (www.kennynnoli.com)

Table of Contents

Dedication

To Mandy:

I continue to enjoy our adventures together. I am thankful that you continue to walk alongside me as we continue to walk in faith together. This book would not be possible without you. You are an amazing mother, wife, friend, and partner.

To Summer & Elijah:

You both continue to teach me every day. I appreciate the way in which you have allowed our home to be open to those who need. I absolutely enjoy watching you grow

I survived cancer when I was 5 years old and I should know that God has a plan for me. I should also know that stories can sometimes be an adventure. I like doing adventures. I am proud that I have a good life, because God has a plan. He always has one and always will.

-Summer Joy Hoggatt

If I could do something about the Church not allowing disabled people in, I would make sure they are allowing disabled people in the church...Mom and Dad, what would you do if the church does not allow disabled people in? I am a very good problem solver and don't give up, so maybe I could help.

-Summer Joy Hoggatt

Beginnings

There are far, far better things ahead than any we leave behind.
C.S. Lewis (Collected Letters of CS Lewis)

Miracles are a retelling in small letters of the very same story which is written across the whole world in letters too large for some of us to see.
C.S. Lewis (God in the Dock)

Journeys & Plans

Journeys have a beginning. In some respects, mine, and subsequently this book's, began in the Summer of 1996. I traveled to Albania to work alongside a team from my college that had been asked to partner with the Education Ministry there. The team consisted of students in the college's special education teacher-prep program, and the director of Special Education for the college. I had no intention of being a special education teacher. All I wanted to be was a history professor. I wanted to read dusty books and talk of times past (something I still immensely enjoy). The truth is that God had other plans. So, largely because I believe they needed someone to carry boxes around, I was invited to join the team. Once we arrived, apart from carrying boxes, I was not entirely useful.

Once in the country, my teammates gave presentations on best practices to native teachers and government officials. During these presentations, I spent time with students at several of the programs, schools, and institutions we visited. Initially, this was not comfortable. Yet, here I was, on a playground with maybe 100 students with varying disabilities. In this context, I was the outsider. I did not look like the students, their teachers, or their families. I could not understand them, as they could not understand me. They and I were just too different.

As is often the way with the things of God, the unexpected occurred. I was sitting in a chair on a dirty and dusty playground at

1

one of the programs the team was at. Seeing me sitting there, two students waved me over to join them. I did not want to go. I would rather have sat there for the next three hours while the team was inside conducting workshops. Yet, I walked over. They wanted me to join them in their soccer game. They talked and pointed, letting me know where they wanted me. I obediently followed along. For the next thirty minutes, we played and laughed. At lunch that day one translator told me their names, Spartak (age 10) and Denis (age 12). Both boys, I was told, were placed in the program because their parents felt the state was the best provider. Both boys were diagnosed with intellectual disabilities and would most likely stay at the program for the greater part of their lives.

For the rest of that day and the two or three days that followed, the two boys stuck to my side. We ate lunch together and played together. As we left that program to head north, I had to say goodbye to the boys.

I had learned a few broken phrases, so I looked at them both and said, "faleminderit," or thank you.

They presented me with drawings they made for me. One was a crayon drawing of a house and the other a picture of Tom & Jerry, signed by the artists.

Then Denis looked at me and said, "do te me mungosh."(Albanian for "I will miss you")

Spartak then hugged me and said, "Unë të dua," (Albanian for "I love you.")

All I could do was hug him back and say the only phrase I knew. "Faleminderit," I replied as tears flowed down my cheeks.

As we drove away, I was overwhelmed with the sense that I had been chosen. I knew what it meant to be chosen. Those two boys chose me. They chose me to be their friend. They chose me to love me. In the world's eyes, they may not have had much to offer. Yet, they were able to give me something I needed.

They chose me.

Everyone wants to be chosen. We want to know that we belong, that we matter to someone.

I keep the pictures they gave me in my office. When I look at the drawings, I smile. I smile because I remember how it feels to be chosen. Also, I am reminded that this gift of choosing is something I can freely give.

Nearly twenty-five years later, I realize that being chosen by two Albanian boys with disabilities put me on a path I am still traveling today. I knew then that God was moving me. I knew that He was choosing and asking me to make different choices. So, after returning from Albania, I moved into a group home for foster youth as a houseparent. Looking back, my career in social services, human services, and education stem from that moment of choosing. That moment of choosing continues to produce results.

As I followed this new path that God laid out for me, I ended up doing social work in Orange, California. While there I met my future wife, Mandy. After Mandy and I had dated for a while, we began to talk about marriage and family. God had placed both of us on a shared journey. As such, it was not a surprise for either of us when we agreed that adoption would be part of our story. We believed that we could not choose otherwise. As we finished our adoption homestudy in September 2008, we did not know how close we were to growing our family. What we learned over the next several

3

months changed our lives forever. Over twelve years later, these lessons continue to shape who we are.

Scars & Hope

The Spring of 2020 presented the world with a disruption never seen before. The Coronavirus pandemic, for many of us changed our plans. Yet, for many of us, COVID-19 brought grief and tragedy into our lives from which many have still not recovered. The pandemic resulted in wounds and scars for people of all ages and stages in their stories. Yet, hope remains, and hope does not disappoint. One thing that resulted in COVID-19 and the social distancing that resulted for me was an opportunity to spend time with my family and to reflect on our story. This book was born out of that time. It is a testament to both scars and hope. The deeper things I learn from God because of the gifts He has placed in my life.

Most mornings, the sweetest blue eyes look at me and say, "Daddy, do you know that I love you."

"Yes," I answer, "I know." Then I wait for what comes next.

"Daddy?" she seems to ask. I feign surprise, as though I did not know the next question was coming fast on the heels of the first. "Do you know that God loves you?"

I nod and smile. "Yes, sweetheart, I do."

Then I ask. "Summer, do you know that God loves you?"

She nods and smiles back, "Yes," is all she says.

I follow with my turn in this ever-constant dance of ours, "how do you know?"

"Because He made me special" She brings her hands into the response as she smiles and continues.

"What do you mean," I ask, knowing the outcome, but excited and expecting, nonetheless.

She smiles and replies in a somewhat exasperated voice as if to say, "If I've told you once, I've told you a million times." She looks me in the eye smiling, "I have scars."

"What do you mean?" I ask once again.

"God is a healer daddy," she says, concluding our routine with finality, knowing there is nothing else to ask once this statement is out there.

Even though I knew this was coming from the beginning, I still get choked up by her response. In a moment, all the emotions of our journey together, all the highs and lows are wrapped up in knowing that God is indeed a healer. That God redeems and heals is something that I should not need to be reminded of, but I welcome the reminder that Summer provides. This is just one example of the many lessons I have learned in Sumer's school of life. So, I respond in the only way that I can as I try to keep tears out of my eyes and my voice. Finally, I smile, look into her eyes, and say, "yes, yes He is."

"The thing is daddy, I'm special," Summer continues matter-of-factly.

Summer does not buy into the worldview she is "special" because she carries a diagnosis of Autism or because she has been labeled as having Intellectual and Developmental Disabilities (IDD). She is not special because she is in "special education." She is not special for any trite or cliched reason. She sees herself as special, in fact, she is special, because God is concerned with her well-being. She is special because the one who created the universe was there for her. The very one who sent His son to die for the world is concerned with Summer's wellbeing.

Summer enjoys telling her story. In fact, it is often the way she introduces herself to others. She will often walk up to people and say, "Hi, I'm Summer Hoggatt. When I was five, I had kidney cancer." Her forthrightness will often take aback people and they will ask, "Are you OK now?"

She will then say, "Yes, because God was there."

Summer is special because she knows, I mean really knows; she does not merely parrot back a response or pay lip-service to an expected answer. Rather, she knows God ~~was~~ is there for her. She believes that God has been there for her and that God will be there for her. It is her scars that serve, not as a token of shame or past trauma, but as an altar of what God did in her life. Summer sees her scars as a gift from which to tell people her story. Her story is a story of healing and redemption. Her scars are a memorial to tell future generations.

The book of Joshua relates the story of how Joshua responded after the LORD held back the waters of the Jordan River so Joshua and the Israelites could cross into the promised land. Joshua had twelve stones taken from the river and set up as a memorial on the west bank of the Jordan. Joshua is clear about the reason. Joshua 4:6-7 (NIV) tells us it was so *"that this may be a sign among you when your children ask in time to come, saying, 'What do these stones mean to you?' Then you shall answer them that the waters of the Jordan were cut off before the ark of the covenant of the LORD; when it crossed over the Jordan, the waters of the Jordan were cut off. And these stones shall be for a memorial to the children of Israel forever."*

As I set out to write this down, Mandy and I have begun anew the process of choosing the path of foster care and adoption. Once again, we face frustration; we face discouragement, and we face fear. Yet, the life of my daughter serves as a memorial. She reminds me to tell the story of what the LORD did. Telling her story encourages me. It quite literally pours courage into me, for I am reminded of what God has done.

God is a healer. The Lord is a deliverer, but we still forget to tell others. Summer does not forget. And because of that, God has used her and her story as a means for pointing others back to Him.

Yes, Summer has scars. She has been wounded in every way imaginable. Summer was born prematurely to a mother who was not able to care for her, and before she spent a single night at "home" she was placed into the care of the local social service agency. From the time she was born until she walked through our doors, she was wounded and scarred. She received scars from being born meth-affected. She received scars from physical, emotional, and sexual abuse at the hands of those who should have taken better care of her. She received scars from well-intentioned adoptive parents who were just not ready to deal with the challenges associated with intellectual and developmental disabilities as well as a diagnosis of autism and sent her back to the "system."

Summer enjoys telling people her story. She is not ashamed or easily embarrassed. I wish I could say that the scarring was something in the past. The truth is, because of the world we live in, we are experiencing wounds regularly, even though some come through well-intentioned messengers. As a father of a child with a disability, I am wounded alongside my daughter when our church Junior High Director lets my family know that the ministry would be better off without her. I am wounded when I overhear comments made to the detriment of my daughter. I am wounded when I experience the struggles she encounters because she learns differently and thinks differently than society expects her to. Yet, I am encouraged when she reminds me that scars are a sign of God's providence. I am encouraged by the way she embraces her story.

Memorials & Lessons

This book serves as a memorial. Not only of Summer's story, but rather how God uses each of our stories to teach. This book is the story of wounds, but it is also the story of healing and perseverance that results in a scar. It is the story of the lessons learned through the scars, the victories, the struggles, the celebrations, and the silences. Yet, it is much more than that. It is the story of pursuit. The pursuit of family, the pursuit of love, and the pursuit of God. Not simply our pursuit of God, though it is that, more importantly it is God's pursuit of us. It is a pursuit of a relationship without knowing who was on the other end of that pursuit. It is not the pursuit of perfection, nor the pursuit of safety. If that were the case, there would be no scars. In most cases, it is the story of how God moved us from what we "wanted" to pursue what He has for us.

Ultimately, this is the story of hope. This is not an empty or shallow hope. This is the story of hope amidst trouble and struggle, yet hope, nonetheless. It is a hope that emanates, not from comfort and luxury, but rather a hope that develops because of scars. Indeed, this is a hope in a personal loving God. A God that provides, that pursues, that welcomes, that gives, and, most importantly, that loves. In Paul's letter to the Romans, he writes:

> "By entering through faith into what God has always wanted to do for us—set us right with him, make us fit for him—we have it all together with God because of our Master Jesus. And that's not all: We throw open our doors to God and discover at the

11

same moment that he has already thrown open his door to us. We find ourselves standing where we always hoped we might stand—out in the wide-open spaces of God's grace and glory, standing tall and shouting our praise."

"There's more to come: We continue to shout our praise even when we're hemmed in with troubles, because we know how troubles can develop passionate patience in us, and how that patience, in turn, forges the tempered steel of virtue, keeping us alert for whatever God will do next. In alert expectancy such as this, we're never left feeling shortchanged. Quite the contrary— we can't round up enough containers to hold everything God generously pours into our lives through the Holy Spirit!" (Romans 5:1-5, MSG)

This is a story of being hemmed in by troubles yet learning through these troubles to lean into God and His faithfulness, goodness, and love. It is the reminders that God pours into our lives so much more than we can ever possibly imagine. So much so, that we cannot "round up enough containers to hold everything God generously pours into our lives." I love that image. There were times in our story when the well felt close to being empty. Sometimes both Mandy and I felt at the end of our rope. Yet, we have learned, and need to be consistently reminded, to remain "alert for whatever God will do next." Why? Because God doesn't shortchange us. In those moments of weary striving, God has regularly and generously poured into our lives in ways that we foolishly failed to expect.

I have the privilege of being a father to two amazing children. I learn from each of them daily. Yet, I have walked alongside Summer for considerably longer than I have walked alongside my son Elijah. As a result, I have learned different lessons from each. So, while I value the lessons I have learned from Elijah, I have spoken into the lessons I have learned in and through the life of my daughter. I have learned what it means to parent—to father—a child labeled with intellectual and developmental disabilities, a child labeled with autism, a child who fought for her life against cancer, a child wounded by a child welfare system meant to protect, but a child who yearns after God's own heart. I have learned how to navigate the challenges that come as part of partially growing up in the child welfare system. I have learned the horrors that come with the helpless feeling of hearing your child has cancer. I have watched God's faithfulness as embodied in the life and story of my daughter. To that end, I have attempted to share Summer's story in a way that honors her, honors our journey, honors our family, but most importantly, honors God. Because, as Paul tells us, "There is more to come."

Choosing & Learning

I am a father, son, professor, brother, husband, friend, and many, many more. I am called, "Daddy," "son," "Mike," "Doctor," "Professor," "Hoggatt," and several other labels, both, in all honesty, good and bad. These are merely roles I play and how people close, and far, identify me. I enjoy some of these roles more than others and appreciate certain labels more than others, typically depending on the person doing the labeling. Some of these labels are attached to familial relationships while others are attached to my professional image. Some are labels I receive because of perceptions people have of me, while still others I receive because of an image I have cultivated. In a sense, I am all these roles and labels while at the same time, none of them, at least completely. I do not like to be pigeonholed into a particular space. I resist it. I am uncomfortable with labels.

It is not that I do not understand the use or practicality of them, it's just that I don't always know where I fit within the labeling scheme. This lack of confidence in my place makes me reluctant to write this book. I do not have an infinity scarf or wear autumn boots or have an evangelically-ish Texas drawl. I work in education and in disability service, so I am often out of place in my affluent ambition-minded suburb of Orange County. After twenty years together, I increasingly see how my Chicana wife struggles to fit into this same white suburban culture. I also see my daughter, beautiful and so full of warmth, struggle to fit into a world in which neurodiverse individuals and people who are not ready for Instagram culture struggle to fit in.

Maybe that is an important aspect of this whole venture. Maybe this is the first lesson. Maybe knowing that we do not fit into this world is the lesson. Maybe it is important that we understand that this disquiet is a sign that we were made for something more. In fact, we were CHOSEN out of this discomfort and placed upon a better path. Yet, it rarely feels this way. In truth, the inability to fit, to find "our place," is associated with feelings of loneliness, anxiety, frustration, and even despair. N.T. Wright refers to this disquiet as an "echo of a voice." This voice calls us back to what was meant to be. In his book, *Simply Christian,* Wright puts it this way, "It's as though we can hear, not perhaps a voice itself, but the echo of a voice: a voice speaking with calm, healing authority, speaking about justice, about things being put to rights, about peace and hope and prosperity for all[1]."

Perhaps the emptiness associated with pursuing success (wealth, intelligence, power) is reflected most starkly in folks like Summer. People who do not fit the world's standard of, well, practically anything. I look at Summer and her life and I think I hear a voice (or the echo of a voice) calling me to hope, calling me to wonder, calling me to courage, calling me to grace, and calling me to live a life closer to my Jesus. Maybe, as Wright reminds us, "The reason we think we have heard a voice is because we have. It wasn't a dream." Summer's life is not the voice, but she reminds me to listen to that voice. She reminds me that it is not all a dream.

It is these very feelings that I hope this book can speak into. Through this book, I hope to share a story of hope from despair and the lessons learned along the way. I am not intending to preach or

---

[1] Wright, N.T. (2006). *Simply Christian. Why Christianity Makes Sense.* Harper Collins: New York.

sermonize. I, like the blind man in John's gospel, am merely trying to convey an encounter with the miraculous.

In John chapter 9:24-27 (NIV) the Pharisees attempt to get the blind man (or formerly blind man) to speak ill of Jesus. In verse 24 they say, "Give glory to God by telling the truth," they said. "We know this man is a sinner."

The blind man replied, "Whether he is a sinner or not, I don't know. One thing I do know. I was blind, but now I see! (25)"

Still, they pressed him for more information, "What did he do to you? How did he open your eyes? (26)"

You can sense both the exasperation and amusement in the blindman's voice, "I have told you already, and you did not listen. (27)" He is letting them know that something miraculous transpired. He cannot explain it, he can only describe it.

I am not attempting to explain why things developed as they did. Like the man in John's gospel, I am simply trying to describe what Jesus did and what He taught. Specifically, I am trying to convey the lessons learned. These lessons I have learned were taught through the life of a young girl with autism and intellectual disabilities. They were taught by a young girl who bravely fought cancer and the child welfare system. They were taught by a young girl who gave me the label of "daddy." A label I have cherished every single day since.

Looking back over the years, I have identified eight lessons learned from life with Summer to share. There are, of course, more lessons to be shared, and more lessons to be learned. Yet, these eight are the ones I feel have the most resonance and meaning, at least for me.

Besides Summer's story, I have also included other thoughts and reflections. As our family walked through foster and adoption and as we walked through cancer, I tried to capture our thoughts through a series of journals and a family blog. I did this both to reflect on our own experience, and as a way of communicating with those involved in our journey. Throughout this book, I have included several entries I feel speak into our experience in meaningful ways. These entries provide a glimpse into my hopes, fears, frustrations, and celebrations as our story unfolded. Sometimes, they remain an accurate reflection of how I continue to think about those events. In other cases, my thinking has changed in the ensuing years. Regardless, these entries labeled as "From the Family Archives" provide an additional lens through which to observe and learn what we experienced as well as what we thought during our journey.

Lessons without application are not worth much. So, I have tried to identify applications of each lesson in a section I have titled, *So What?*. These brief sections following the lessons build upon the work of an author that has moved, encouraged, or convicted me in my walk as those works connect to the identified lesson.

In *Loss is part of the story, but not THE story*, I have tried to unpack the truth that despite the made-for-television mystic that adoptions often have within the wider Christian community, all adoptions begin with loss. I have tried to honor that loss by sharing part of Summer's journey through loss into adoption. I have also tried to emphasize that while loss is part of the story, God writes a larger story wherein that loss is redeemed and remembered as a part of the story, for sure, but not the whole story.

In *when the way seems hopeless, but God. . .*, I explain how God has worked within Summer's story to show that God is bigger, immeasurably so, than our fears. The grief, loss, pain, disappointment, and heartache we experience in this life, while real, when seen in the light of God's strength, mercy, and grace take on a different meaning and impact in our own lives.

In *we were made to belong* I get to share about the joy, and struggle, of finally getting to build a forever family with Summer Joy. However, I also talk to the challenges faced by individuals labeled with disabilities as they too often face rejection and marginalization at the hands of those who should be embracing them with open arms.

The urgent things are not always the essential things is a lesson Jesus proclaims in Bethany at the house of Mary and Martha. It is also a truth that I could never have learned in academia or in the hustle and bustle of the modern world. Rather, it is a lesson learned from a cancer-surviving, foster care surviving, girl labeled with intellectual disabilities and autism.

Grace and Gratitude are choices. This chapter describes how living with a child who has experienced early drug exposure and child abuse and who struggles to understand a world that does not readily accommodate her own unique way of thinking and being requires a capacity for Grace only God provides. Yet, learning that I need and am required to extend Grace intentionally is something I can learn to be grateful for. I also am learning how to be grateful for the things that I had not noticed until Summer spoke them into my life.

Fear Not is a lesson learned from the bravest individual I have ever met. Summer's ability to be courageous in the face of danger is a lesson unto itself. This lesson is not about minimizing danger or ignoring the challenges that countless many experiences every day. It is not about ignoring the pain that individuals impacted by the child welfare system or affected by disabilities know and live out daily. Rather, it is about knowing a God that is larger still.

There is beauty to be found, is a lesson that I could never have learned on my own. The perspective to look, to seek, to purposeful identify, the beauty is what that lesson is about. This chapter isn't about defining beauty, nor is it about reacting to beauty. Rather this is about looking for the fingerprint of God in the world and recognizing that God is a God beauty, real beauty.

The things of God are ALWAYS worth the wait. Time can be such an enemy to so many of us. This lesson was a reminder to me that God is not a God of disappointment. Waiting for the hopes and dreams we each have can feel overwhelming, yet this chapter reminds us that not only does God not disappoint, but the things God promises are always, always worth the wait.

My prayer is that you can benefit from the lessons I have learned. I have endeavored to share those lessons to the best of my ability with as much accuracy as I can, given the passing of time. My prayer also is that regardless of where you are, or how you identify, there is something for you to learn as well. Regardless, I appreciate your time as I share with you a little of our story.

I remember waiting for Summer's arrival, though at the time we did not know who Summer was. The one thing I did know was that I was scared. I felt woefully under-prepared. I had questions about what kind of father I would be. I had questions on how this new addition would impact my relationship with my wife. I was anxious, excited, worried, afraid, and unaware. I did not have the slightest inkling of the great many things I would learn because of following this road. Of choosing this path. This book is an attempt to express or describe the many important things I learned because of choosing to follow God in this adventure. This book explains how those lessons were taught through the life of my, now teenage, daughter Summer.

I center much of this book around our story of adoption with our daughter Summer. Within this story, there are several opportunities where choosing, or the choices, are abundantly clear. Yet, the important choices were not the ones that Mandy and I made. Rather, they are the ones that Summer made. They are the "choosings" that two Albanian boys with disabilities made. They are the choices God makes that are so radically different from the choices we are too often tempted to make on who belongs and who can be useful. So, the lessons, I attempt to identify in this book, are ultimately the result of choices I have observed in my daughter. Her choice to choose courage over fear. To choose welcome over exclusion. To choose wonder over cynicism. To choose joy over sorrow. To choose hope over despair. To choose grace and gratitude and not rejection. To choose love.

From the Family Archives:

Waiting with Fear and Trembling (Summer 2008)

Right now, it seems like there is nothing for us to do but wait. We have completed the classes we need to and have submitted our application for adoption. Until our assigned adoption worker contacts us with the next step in the process, we have nothing left to do, but wait. Waiting is never easy, and it allows the opportunity for anxiety and fear to creep into our lives. I have been worrying lately whether my son or daughter, to be, will call me "dad," or "daddy." Mandy and I have chosen to build our family through adoption, but what if the child we choose does not choose us? I'm not sure how I would feel if the young boy I call "son" chose to call me "Mr. Hoggatt." How would I handle it if the young girl I called "daughter" called me "Mike?" I realize that they are not the most rational of fears and that the well-being and happiness of our child are what's important, but I cannot pretend that I do not think about this from time to time.

It is true that we plan on providing all of these things that parents are expected to provide, yet this is not guaranteed to elicit affection from a child. People will assure me if our child realizes how much we went through to adopt and how much we wanted our son or daughter to come and be a part of our family. Yet, I know from first-hand experience that this is not the case.

The word "Abba," in the gospel, is used to indicate the type of relationship we should have with our heavenly father. When we pray, Christ says, call your Heavenly Father, "Daddy." How seldom do I even call upon my heavenly father? He has chosen to adopt me when logic dictates that He shouldn't. He has chosen to lavish on me an inheritance I do not deserve. He has given me more through the adoption He offers, than I could ever dream of giving the son or daughter I want to adopt. Still, I fail to call on Him as I should. I fail to see Him as the father He is. I fail to demonstrate my affection, respect, and love for Him. I want to, but like St. Paul says, I don't do what I know I should. In light of the adoption relationship I share with my Heavenly Father, why should I expect my adopted child to respond to me in a more loving and affectionate fashion than I respond to my adoptive Father? Yet, the more and more I think about it, the less anxious or worried I am. Of the many gifts, my Heavenly Father has given to me is Hope, and hope that is placed in God does not disappoint.

This adoption is all about Hope. From our future son or daughter, there is an unspoken hope for a family that will provide a Home with all the love, hope, joy, happiness, and strength a child deserves. For Mandy and I there is a Hope that God will place the child we have been waiting for since before we met. There is a hope that people will see our son and daughter as family, not "adoptive-family." One of the great things about this whole process is the Hope that is so integral to it all. All the hoops and hurdles, obstacles and barriers, poor trainers and difficult systems are easier because of hope. I know that, apart from not venturing into this process, we would never be able to keep going if we did not have hope. Not just any hope, but a hope placed in a loving God who happens to be an expert in adoption.

Lessons

Do not be influenced by the importance of the writer, and whether his learning be great or small, but let the love of pure truth draw you to read. Do not inquire, Who said this? but pay attention to what is said.

Thomas a Kempis (The imitation of Christ)

Lesson #1: Loss is part of the story, but it is not THE Story

Early in Charles Dickens, "A Christmas Carol," the narrator informs the audience that *"There is no doubt that Marley was dead. This must be distinctly understood, or nothing wonderful can come of the story I am going to relate."* For the ghost story that follows to be fantastic or wonderful, we must first acknowledge that Marley is dead.

In much the same way we might also be forgiven for saying, *"There is no doubt that adoption begins with loss. This must be distinctly understood, or nothing wonderful can come of the story I am going to relate."* OK, not exactly Dickensian. Yet, I think it serves as a telling glimpse into what is to come. Every single story of adoption begins with loss. There are no exceptions. A child who is adopted must first encounter loss. Somehow something is not as it "should" be. Perhaps a tragedy has removed the parents from the picture. Or perhaps abuse or neglect has caused the loss. There are any number of culprits to blame for the loss: drugs, alcohol, anger, selfishness, etc. The point is that without loss there would be no need for adoption. The same can be said of our adoption in Christ. Paul writes in Galatians 4:4-5 (NIV) that "God sent his Son, born of a woman, born under the law, to redeem those under the law, that we might receive adoption." Again, would this be necessary if we weren't lost?

I think too often our society, particularly the church, celebrates adoptions and fostering without acknowledging the loss that has occurred. It could be the loss of family, loss of life, loss of fertility, loss of safety, loss of rights, loss of childhood, or even the loss of country. Regardless, I do not advocate that we dwell on the loss. However, I do believe that the loss is part of the story, and by ignoring that part of the story we do not honor the individual for whom this is their story. Summer's story begins with loss.

SUMMER'S STORY [2]

In January 2005, Samantha Hernandez was pregnant and scared. A young woman in her early twenties with some enormous obstacles in her path, not the least of these was her addiction to methamphetamines. She had just been arrested for the second time in six months for methamphetamine use. Now she sat in a sterile room within the county jail facility waiting on her service coordinator assigned through the state Department of Developmental Services because of a diagnosis of Intellectual and Developmental Disabilities. Accompanying the service coordinator was a representative from the county child welfare agency. The purpose of the visit was to check on Samantha's well-being, but also to inform her that her child would be removed from her custody once delivered, and would remain in the care of the courts until such a time that either Samantha or her on-again/off-again boyfriend, Jonathan could complete a court-ordered reunification plan. At this same time, Jona-

---

[2] Neither Mandy nor I were there for most of this story. However, I have recreated the scenes based on an abundance of court papers as well as interviews with county workers familiar with the case. As such, I can say with confidence that this is a reliable account of the events presented here.

than, who had been diagnosed with paranoid schizophrenia, had been placed in the county psychiatric facility after a recent arrest.

Samantha had previously been given a treatment plan to mitigate the ill-affects her child might experience because of her lifestyle. This plan included treatment for meth use as well as prescriptions and regular prenatal care designed to support both mother and prospective child. Samantha had refused to complete any of the recommended steps to care for herself and her child. As a result, they informed Samantha at this meeting that her child would most likely suffer a variety of complications and struggle to have a decent quality of life.

Armed with this information, the state and county worker let Samantha know that she would be within her rights if she chose to terminate the pregnancy. However, Samantha might have been deemed unfit to provide the care required for her own child, yet she was deemed fit to make decisions for her own body. She defiantly informed the professionals involved in her case that she was carrying her child to term. Despite the protestations of the professionals, they had no choice, but to agree.

A few months later, on a mid-April morning, a full two months before the expected delivery date, Samantha delivered an underweight, premature girl struggling to live. Immediately, the child was whisked away to the neonatal intensive care unit (NICU), but not before Samantha had a chance to give the little girl a name. Thus, Summer entered the world.

Summer would spend the next two months as a resident of Children's Hospital of Orange County (placement #1) struggling to live. Once she was sufficiently stable, the county social welfare agency found a foster family to provide care (placement #2). Meanwhile, the county had a legal obligation to search for a kinship (or relative) placement understanding that family placements are best situated to meet the developmental needs of a child in care. So, after a few months with the first foster family, Summer was placed into the care of a maternal aunt (her biological mother's sister) and uncle (placement #3). The county placing agency was excited by this placement. First, it was a family placement, which fulfilled a legal mandate. Second, it was in the city of Long Beach, which, while only a few miles away, had the advantage of being in another county, and, therefore, "another county's "problem."

Summer would celebrate her first birthday with this new "family." Yet, unbeknownst to those charged with her welfare, Summer was not receiving the care and support she required. The home was a virtual revolving door of drug abusers and other disreputable visitors. What the county placing agency did not know, or did not bother to know, was that this home was a known heroin den. During this time, Summer was abused in every way imaginable, and some that should not be imagined. Finally, during a raid by the local police, Summer was found in this home. She was found in her own filth, surrounded by needles and users. Law enforcement immediately took her into care and placed her into Los Angeles County receiving (placement #4).

Upon placement, Los Angeles County identified that Summer should have rightfully been placed back into the care of Orange County Social Services So, once again, Summer was placed into a local Orange County emergency foster home (placement #5). Emergency Foster Homes are short-term placements that allow the local welfare agency to find something more stable and/or more permanent. So, within a few days, a suitable foster home (placement #6) was found that could respond to Summer's needs while the courts figured out what to do next.

However, despite some obvious delays in her speech, gross motor development, and cognition, the courts were optimistic that a permanent placement would help to improve these delays. So, Summer was placed into a potential adoptive family. In the state of California, a family must foster a child for at least six months before an adoption can be finalized. This is assuming that all parental rights have been revoked, and the child is legally freed for adoption. In Summer's case, she was legally freed for adoption, so the placement occurred shortly after her second birthday. So it was that Summer came to live with John and Lori Wainwright (placement #7).

As you might imagine. A child born meth-affected, who has been placed into six different homes by their second birthday, would most likely not be a well-adjusted, or an easy child. Unfortunately, John and Lori expected her to be both easy and well-adjusted. Previously, John and Lori had experienced trouble conceiving and looked to the county for a child to add to their family. Lori hoped this addition might heal their marriage and divert the couple from their existing troubles. John went along, thinking this would please his wife and, after all, she would do much of the heavy lifting of child rearing, so what could be the harm. So, Summer's placement was initially met with welcome by both John and Lori.

Summer's placement with the family was rough from the beginning. Summer's behaviors were difficult to deal with, nor were the extreme delays she exhibited. The delays prompted the question of origin. Were these delays caused by the drugs? Were they caused by the multiple placements? Were they genetic? They were most likely a combination of the above. Regardless of their cause, John and Lori were not prepared to support Summer's needs. Summer wasn't walking, and she wasn't speaking. Rather, she crawled and barked. She failed to demonstrate basic cognitive milestones expected of a child approaching thirty months.

Gradually, John distanced himself from his spouse. Slowly he began staying later and later at the office. He found excuse after excuse to stay away from the home, from his wife, from Summer. Over time Lori was forced with a choice, the child or her marriage. She knew that she could not raise Summer alone, and, when she was perfectly honest with herself, she had to admit that she really did not want to. So, she contacted Summer's court appointed social worker and returned Summer back to the care of the child welfare agency. Summer was immediately placed with another waiting foster family (placement #8).

After the failed adoption placement, a decision was made to provide Summer with a more stable environment before looking at what was the best long-term plan for Summer. So, around Summer's third birthday, she was placed in a group home with five other children of various ages (placement #9). The group home was part of a collective of homes in an isolated neighborhood in an off-the-beaten-path area of South Orange County. In Summer's home there were five other residents of which she was the youngest, as well as the three children of the group home "parents" who lived in the home and provided some staffing. Summer lived in the group home for six months before the courts decided that her case, and potential adoptive placements, should be reviewed. During her time in the group home, Summer's behaviors had stabilized. They were still problematic, but much more predictable. Also, her language had improved as she was gaining more words receptively and adding a few more words to her expressive vocabulary. Although her expressive language was still limited, maybe twenty-five words, she was communicating in other ways with visitors and group home staff.

If the story ends here, there would be little wonderful to relate. Yet, while all adoptions begin with loss, that is not the end of every story.

Despite the gains made in her new placement, Summer still had challenges, and any potential placement would have to be able to accept and support those challenges. Several individuals involved in her case did not think she was prepared to be placed on an adoption track so soon. However, during her time in the group home, Summer was assigned a new caseworker, Leslie. Leslie understood the reality that every day over two years of age that a child lived in placement, their chances of being adopted decreased significantly. Coupled with her unique developmental challenges, Summer was reaching the point in which the courts would deem her "unadoptable" and make plans to keep her in residential care until she emancipated at eighteen or twenty-one. So, in September 2008, Leslie made efforts to have Summer placed into a forever family.

Despite some pushback from her colleagues and supervisor cautioning her against an attempt to match Summer with a prospective family, Leslie went forward and submitted Summer's case to the adoption's department. Within two weeks, Leslie began preparing to present Summer's case to a prospective family.

From the Family Archives (Spring 2007)

Well, tonight Mandy and I will be attending the Adoption Application Workshop required by Orange County Social Services. While we have attended adoption orientations through both our local social service agency and a private domestic agency, tonight begins a more focused season in our adoption process. I've decided to keep a record of our adoption process as we go, but I wanted to provide a little background.

Sometime in mid-2006, we both concluded that adoption was right for us. We had talked about this prior to getting married and during the first several years of our marriage, but always as a possibility. By Thanksgiving 2006 we came to adoption as a reality. We told our families around Christmas 2006 and proceeded from there. . .

I know my son or daughter is out there waiting for me. They may or may not yet be born, or even conceived, but they are out there. There is not a day that goes by that I don't wander about them. I'm nervous and excited. There is an excitement of knowing that every hoop we jump through and every form we fill out will bring us one step closer to the making of our family. We still don't know for sure if we will stick with the County Social Services or decide to go through a private domestic agency, but God does and we are confident that He will lead us to exactly the place our son or daughter is waiting.

At the beginning of the fifteenth chapter of Luke's gospel, the Pharisees are incensed that Jesus would welcome sinners and tax collectors. Jesus responds to the Pharisees' indignation by telling three stories. Each story illustrates the overwhelming love and welcome of God. There is the story of a lost sheep. The good shepherd leaves the ninety-nine to track down that which was lost. Not only does He pursue the lost sheep, but He rejoices once the sheep is found.

Next, we meet a woman who has lost a few coins. She scours the house. She is looking, searching, pursuing those lost coins. Once she finds the coins, she cannot help it, she has to tell someone. Her joy at finding what was lost is so great that she cannot hold party in isolation—it must be shared.

Finally, Jesus tells the story of the prodigal son. The son is "lost" in a moral/spiritual sense. The father stands on the road looking for his son. Even while he "was still a long way off," the father is moved with compassion, runs to his son, and embraces him. Again, once the lost has been found, recovered, and redeemed, there is a party. There is joy that comes when holy redemption meets the deep longing of our soul.

Our story starts with loss. Before you or I arrived on the planet, humanity was lost. We were lost sheep. We were a few coins. We were a prodigal seeking our own way. Yet, our story does not end there.

During the US Civil War many Union Officer Prisoners of War were kept in Libby Prison in Richmond, Virginia. Libby Prison was notorious for malnutrition, physical abuse, and generally poor living conditions experienced by the POWs. Following his release from Libby Prison, Henry L. Gilmore had a clearer understanding of what it meant to leave darkness, isolation, and loss in order to be embraced into the welcome of love. In reflection he wrote the following hymn as an expression of his own experience with the unending, unrelenting, searching and saving love of God.

When out in sin, and darkness lost, Love found me;

My fainting soul was tempest toss'd, Love found me;

I heard the Savior's words so blest, Love found me;

Come weary, heavy laden rest, Love found me.

Oh, 'twas love, love

Love that moved the mighty God,

Love, love, 'twas love found me[3]*.*

We have all experienced loss. At one time or another we will be face to face with loss. Some losses have a greater impact than others. We mourn the loss of a marriage that has been sacrificed on the altar of self. We mourn the loss of health or life as the great enemy, Cancer, comes for us or the ones we love. We mourn the loss of family as one we love is led away in chains for choices they would rather take back. We mourn the loss of self as we survive in toxic relationships. There are more losses. Each loss is meaningful to the person who has experienced the loss. Each person mourns in their own way. There are losses particular to different groups. For families impacted by disability there are often losses mourned due to the drifting apart of family and/or friendship groups.

---

[3] Gilmore, H. L. (1890). "Love Found Me." Public Domain.

Emily Peri Kingsley, who spent nearly forty-five years writing for Sesame Street writes in *Welcome to Holland* of the loss of expectation when a child is born with disabilities. These too are losses to be mourned. Kingsley explains that raising a child with a disability is like planning a trip to Italy. As you plan, you look forward to Venice, Rome, Milan, and Florence. You anticipate visiting the Coliseum and Sistine Chapel. It is all very exciting. Yet, on the day of your departure, after months of planning and excitement, you are greeted at the airport with a sign that says, "Welcome to Holland." You know that you are supposed to be in Italy. However, the truth is that Holland has beautiful things, like Tulips, Windmills, and Rembrandts. Still, Kingsley explains, *"everyone you know is busy coming and going to Italy. They are bragging about the excitement, while you look around at the slower-paced life in Holland, thinking that Italy was where you were supposed to go."*

She concludes her narrative with:

> *"And the pain of that will never, ever, ever, ever go away... because the loss of that dream is a very, very significant loss. But...if you spend your life mourning the fact that you didn't get to go to Italy, you may never be free to enjoy the very special, the very lovely things... about Holland[4]."*

I would be lying if I were to state that all losses are redeemed in this life. Or that the pain from the loss somehow goes away. Our evidence, our experience, lets us know that this is simply not true. However, we can take courage. Why? Because we have been promised that "There's more to come" so "We continue to shout our praise even when we're hemmed in with troubles" staying "alert for

---

[4] Emily Peri Kingsley. (1987). Welcome to Holland. © All Rights Reserved.

whatever God will do next. In alert expectancy such as this, we're never left feeling shortchanged." We are not left feeling shortchanged, because God is a God of hope.

In my time with my daughter, I have learned one thing above others. Yes, there is loss in this life, but God is a God of redemption. God is a God that redeems the wasted years so that, as the prophet Joel proclaims the word of the LORD, "[We]'ll know without question that I'm in the thick of life with Israel, That I'm your God, yes, your God, the one and only real God. Never again will my people be despised." (Joel 2:27, MSG)

Yes, God is a God in whom we can place our Hope. We can hope and not despair over the lost things. We know that as shepherds look for lost sheep, and women scour the house for a few small coins, and fathers embrace their prodigal children, we are confident that God pursues us as well. In short, there is loss in our story, but that is never, never, never the end of the story. As I learn this lesson and lean into this lesson, the road ahead looks better and brighter.

Yet, as I write this, I have been losing battles left and right. I have hit roadblocks advocating for Summer's school. My wife has struggled with her health. Our church has told us that Summer is not welcomed to worship with the High School ministry. I feel that I should be victorious. I promised my daughter when she came into my life that I would fight for her. I would fight battles for her and with her. Part of me feels that every battle should be easily won. In my moments of honesty, I know that is not the world in which I live. Still, I feel powerless as Mandy goes to doctor appointment after doctor appointment with no answers. I feel powerless when Summer is still shut out of the things her mother and I want so desperately for her. I am discouraged. I am frustrated. I am angry. I feel lost.

Maybe recognizing my weakness, my sense of being lost, is the first step toward being found. Maybe God is reminding me that the battle belongs to the LORD, and not to me. Maybe I am simply learning to be faithful in the losing. After all, the Master does not commend his servants for being successful or victorious. Rather, "The master said, 'Well done, my good and faithful servant. You have been faithful in handling this small amount, so now I will give you many more responsibilities. Let's celebrate together!'" (Matthew 25:23 NLT) So, I will try to be good and faithful, but the LORD knows I need a lot of work.

Despite the struggles, despite the obstacles, I am confident that the losses do not define us. Recently, Mandy and I had been having conversations with Elijah and Summer regarding the process we were embarking on to become licensed as a foster/adoptive placement known as a Resource Family. We had explained to both that their prospective brother or sister might come into our family with a variety of needs. They asked why, and we explained the reasons why a child might be in the foster care system and why they might have heightened needs as a result.

Then Summer looked at us and said, "Am I a foster child?"

"No Summer," I told her. "You were a foster child, but now you are my girl." She then leaned over and put her head on my shoulder and gave me a squeeze. Summer has known that she was adopted. She knows the process, as we have discussed it at length with her. She loves her story and will relay it with relish, albeit a little too frequently at times.

Summer is not confused about who she is, though she may at times be confused about the labels. But labels are a tricky thing. As is identity.

There is probably nothing that makes me smile as wide as when Summer says, with as much exacerbation as she can muster, "daaaadddyy." It is a canned response to a joke or a bit of sarcasm from me. It is her way of letting me know that she knows that I am full of baloney. It is also her way of saying that things are OK. She only says "daddy" in that way when everything is good. When things are not so good, she uses a variety of other methods to let me know that things are not square with us. Most notably she will point a finger (no, not that finger) and call me "you" or Mandy and I "you guys." Once that comes out, we know we are in for a struggle. But "daddy" is something else. Something that is just mine, that comes from just her. Sure, Elijah says "daddy," but he does so in a way that is also uniquely his.

That is true about most parents. We know our child's voice and they know ours. This knowledge can be of the greatest comfort, or it can be of the utmost terror. Yet, the knowledge of that voice persists.

Mandy, Elijah, Summer and I were sitting in the waiting room of our dentist. As is the case with most of our routine visits, Summer knows and is known by all the staff. Summer wandered up to the front desk and began a conversation with the receptionist.

"I am going to a special camp," she says.

40

"Oh really, that's nice," comes the polite reply.

"It's a camp for kids like me," she pauses as if to add emphasis and then clearly articulates each syllable as she continues, "kids with dis-a-bil-i-ties."

Summer has worn her share of labels in her lifetime. She carries a label of autism. She carries a label of intellectual disability. She is not ashamed to be disabled. She does not hide from that label. When much of society is ashamed or runs from the word "disability" she embraces it. Why? I believe it is because Summer understands that disability reflects the world and the barriers she faces. But the labels do not define her.

She has been a foster child. She is a cancer survivor. She wears the labels of Autism and Intellectual Disability. She even fancies herself a Paleontologist in training. Yet, what I learn from Summer is that regardless of the labels we may wear, or the losses we have experienced, they are not our identity. Our identity is deeply held in the arms of those who love us. Of those who know our true labels. Our most important identity is that we are part of the family of God. And He knows our name.

According to John's gospel (20:1), Mary Magdalene went to the tomb on Sunday morning and saw that someone had removed the stone. She then tells Peter and John. She must have been frantic as she cries, in verse two "They have taken the Lord out of the tomb, and we don't know where they have put him! (20:2, NIV)" Peter and John do a cursory inspection (there is great imagery of the younger John arriving first yet reluctant to enter while the more desperate

Peter barges straight in) they return to "where they were staying." (20:9 NIV)

Mary Magdalene, meanwhile, remained near the tomb. We cannot be sure why she stayed behind. However, we know that the absence of Jesus troubled her.

John 20:11-16 (NIV) picks up the story:

> *Now Mary stood outside the tomb crying. As she wept, she bent over to look into the tomb and saw two angels in white, seated where Jesus' body had been, one at the head and the other at the foot.*
>
> *They asked her, "Woman, why are you crying?"*
>
> *"They have taken my Lord away," she said, "and I don't know where they have put him." At this, she turned around and saw Jesus standing there, but she did not realize that it was Jesus.*
>
> *He asked her, "Woman, why are you crying? Who is it you are looking for?"*
>
> *Thinking he was the gardener, she said, "Sir, if you have carried him away, tell me where you have put him, and I will get him."*
>
> *Jesus said to her, "Mary."*
>
> *She turned toward him and cried out in Aramaic, "Rabboni!" (which means "Teacher").*

Did you catch that? She is crying. Her eyes may be swollen from the tears shed over the past two days. She may have difficulty seeing clearly through the early morning light. Regardless of the reason, she does not recognize Jesus. We know from other gospel accounts of

Jesus' post-resurrection appearances that He was visibly different. There was something unrecognizable about Him. Even His closest friends (see John 21) failed to recognize Him immediately. It should not be surprising that Mary Magdalene, despite her love for Jesus, would fail to recognize Him.

The Angels ask her why she is crying. She tells them that her Lord has been taken. She turns around and does not recognize Jesus standing in front of her. Again, this is understandable given the myriad of reasons. She even talks with Him. He calls her "woman" and she thinks He is the gardener. She does not recognize that voice. "This isn't the name my Lord calls me," she thinks. She knows in her heart that her Lord knows her in a deep and meaningful way. So, when Jesus calls her "Mary" everything changes. That is her name. That is her Lord. She would recognize the way He calls her anywhere. Everything changes. Tears of bitter loneliness turn to joyful exclamation. She is not some crying woman. She is Mary. Her identity is intimately wrapped up in that of her Lord, so when He calls her, she responds. Her morning started with loss, but like ours the loss did not remain, nor was it allowed to define.

Loss is part of the story, but it is not THE Story: Now What?

"Compassion is not bending toward the underprivileged from a privileged position; it is not a reaching out from on high to those who are less fortunate below; it is not a gesture of sympathy or pity for those who fail to make it in the upward pull. On the contrary, compassion means going directly to those people and places where suffering is most acute and building a home there." Henri Nouwen[5].

The above quote lies at the heart of how we must respond to loss. We take up residence and build our home amongst the loss, as Nouwen did by leaving the confines of academia and going to live in relationship alongside individuals with developmental disabilities. In the US alone, there are tens of thousands of children whose stories are full of the loss that Summer knew, that she remembers, that continues to influence her development and journey. There are families struggling to understand the loss of expectation, the loss of future, and the loss of hope amid an unexpected diagnosis. Sure, loss may not be the WHOLE story, but it is a part that we as believers, as individuals dealing with our own loss(es), must learn to grapple with. So, what do we do in response to these losses?

---

[5] Nouwen, H. J. M. (2017). *You are the Beloved: Daily Meditations for Spiritual Living.* Hachette UK.

We could minimize it. We could dismiss it. Both options allow us to move forward and pretend that all is perfectly well. Just as problematic is the tendency, particularly in the American Christian culture is to become a tourist in the loss of others. We visit. We take five days to treat foster youth like royalty, but then go about our lives for the other 360 days of the year. The individuals labeled with disabilities who have been marginalized, disrespected, abused, and mistreated experience loss. Yet, the loss-tourist spends one "night to remember" with these individuals, then goes about their own life. Do not get me wrong, I am not opposed to volunteer work or short-term mission work. Yet, that work, that opportunity can either provide the self-satisfaction the loss-tourist experiences full of memories and mementos of another place. Or, that work can create the impetus to build home amongst the loss.

So, what does taking up residence and building a home look like in the everyday? I think there are three major differences between how loss-tourists experience the world compared to those who take up residence.

LOSS-TOURISTS DISMISS THE LOSS. RESIDENTS HONOR THE LOSS.

Denying the loss serves no one. Rather, we honor and show respect by validating that loss, by acknowledging the pain that accompanies that loss, and stepping into that loss alongside those who experience that loss. In fact, when we step into that loss, we show that God is not through with the story.

Nowhere is this more readily demonstrated than when we dare to enter the brokenness experienced by those impacted by the child welfare system. Jason Johnson, author of *Reframing Foster*, writes of his family's experience navigating through the US child welfare system and of God's ability to redeem loss. He claims "[t]he beauty of foster care is showcased against the backdrop of the brokenness that surrounds it[6]." In other words, ignoring the loss does not honor the individual or the God who redeems. Moreover, Johnson argues that the loss, the hurt, the poverty, and the brokenness are nothing to be ashamed of. He writes, "[i]n the gospel our poverty is no longer a source of shame but rather the platform upon which the sufficiency and abundance of God can be made most visible." We honor the loss and the brokenness not by celebrating it nor by minimizing it. Rather, we honor it by acknowledging and giving it to the God who redeems all loss. We honor the journey and the story of each one by putting things in their proper perspective.

LOSS-TOURISTS VISIT THE PAIN AND LOSS RESIDENTS DIG IN.

We further honor each other's stories when we choose the road of compassion. Compassion, as Nouwen rightly claims, is not about healing the broken, for that is for God's. Rather, it is about changing our mindset from one fixated on outcomes and measures of success to one in which our goal is faithfulness on the road of com-

---

[6] Johnson, J. (2018). *Reframing Foster Care: Filtering Your Foster Parenting Journey Through the Lens of the Gospels.* Credo Publishing: Grand Rapids, Michigan.

passion. Here Johnson argues, "[y]our success as a foster parent isn't measured by your capacity to produce some certain set of outcomes; it's determined by your willingness to be faithful along the way and to trust that in the beauty, struggle, joy, and heartache of it all the journey is worth it, that Jesus is beautiful—and that so is what you are doing for these kids."

Again, the truth of the gospel demands that we build a home alongside those in need. Alongside those who have suffered loss. There is no better ground on which to build than alongside those impacted by the child welfare system. Johnson speaks of the privilege we have to build a home in this broken and barren land. He writes, "[i]n light of the gospel it's our privilege to crawl into the story of others, to wrap ourselves in their brokenness and willingly be broken by it—to exchange our normal for theirs and so begin to craft an entirely new and better normal together." For the truth of the gospel changes our expectations. We no longer aim for minor successes. Nor is our expectation that we will be blessed and win acclaim from our peers. The simple expectation is one in which all things will be well. Johnson again speaking to the redemption story of foster and adoption opportunities states it so well: "The expectation isn't that your love will always pull people out of a broken place but that it will at least be willing to walk with them in and through it."

LOSS-TOURISTS ARE BUSY WRITING THEIR NAME ON THE LOSS.
RESIDENTS GIVE THE LOST BACK THEIR NAME.

As Mary sat weeping in the garden, the savior spoke her name. I imagine that He whispered the way only one who deeply cares for another can. We can respond to loss in a like manner. As adoptive parents, Mandy and I could give Summer Joy Hoggatt a new name. A name that changed the complexion and the direction of her story, and ours.

When we enter the story, God writes for us we exchange dirty robes for royal ones. This great exchange that God orchestrates is something we can take part in. We can exchange labels. We can exchange lost and abandoned for loved and pursued. We can exchange worthless and broken for redeemed and valued. We can exchange orphaned and rejected for welcomed and loved. This is nothing new, for we who call ourselves followers of Christ understand that "[t]he good news for all of us is that the gospel has the unique ability to transform costs into privileges and inconveniences into opportunities."

The question is: why wait? There are individuals like Summer waiting for someone to enter their story. To honor their loss, build a home in their hurt, and give them a new, redeemed name. Yet, countless many sit in the comfort of their secure and stable lives waiting and afraid to enter that loss. Here Jason Johnson sums up the opportunity of foster and adoption care nicely, "When all is said and done, let's talk less about what it will cost us to foster or adopt and more time talking about what it will cost these kids if we don't."

Unfortunately, the loss-tourist is unconcerned with that question. They are unwilling to enter the challenge or the difficulty. Of course, it is difficult. Summer's story was and continues to be, a challenge. Yet, her story reminds me I would be a fool to reject what God offers. The story we enter when we enter the loss of another is a horror story, action-adventure, at times, a comedy, but always, a love story. Residents understand the power of this love story while acknowledging the pain and difficulty. Only homebuilders, like Jason Johnson, looking back on his own journey through foster and adoption can say, "[i]t is the mercy of God that He doesn't show us everything that will unfold in the foster care and adoption journey the moment we first say yes to it. All the hard would be too unbearable and all the good would be too unbelievable."

Lesson #2: When the way seems hopeless, but God. . .

The world can overwhelm us. A cancer diagnosis silences our hopes and seeks to steal our joy. A confession of adultery shakes our family, our identity, our future. A prison sentence separates us from the ones we love. Abuse leaves long term emotional scars. Financial hardships bring despair for the future. Relationships don't work out. Friendships fall apart. Jobs fail. Grand expectations are unmet. Simple promises remain undelivered. Our world comes to a crashing halt because of a virus. Regardless of the circumstance, we still face the unmet expectation or the unmet promise. As long as our hopes are based in this world it is easy to despair. Yet, I remind you of what Paul said to us

> *By entering through faith into what God has always wanted to do for us—set us right with him, make us fit for him—we have it all together with God because of our Master Jesus. And that's not all: We throw open our doors to God and discover at the same moment that he has already thrown open his door to us. We find ourselves standing where we always hoped we might stand—out in the wide-open spaces of God's grace and glory, standing tall and shouting our praise. (Romans 5:1-4, MSG)*

When I was a child, before I was told that worship music needed smoke machines and bass drums, I sang a song about my God being so big and so mighty that there was nothing He could not do. I think in the years between my childhood and my encounter with Summer; I forgot that simple, yet mighty truth.

In California, an adoptive parent must also be licensed as a foster parent. This prolongs the process and requires multiple individuals to check-off the place of residence. At the time, Mandy and I were living in a small two-bedroom apartment in Brea, California. We had made a commitment to be as open as possible to whatever child God had intended for us. So, we set up as neutral a room as we could (no pinks or blues). We placed a toddler bed in the room and had a twin bed waiting should we need to swap one out. With that in mind, we believed this to be an "all-ages" bedroom. The licensing individual from the county foster care agency looked at our paperwork and then looked at the bedroom. "It says on your paperwork that you are open to placements from birth to eighteen," she said.

"Yes, that is correct." we responded.

"So, where is the twin bed?" she asked rather brusquely. Then continued, "A five-year-old can't be expected to sleep in a crib."

Sheepishly, we told her that my sister had one available, but we didn't want to overcrowd the apartment. We figured that once we knew the age of the child, we could, within hours, swap for the appropriate bed.

"Since the bed isn't here, I can't license you for any child older than two years," She responded as she continued the review.

We were stunned. We knew that most waiting children were older than two years of age. We didn't know what to do, so we prayed. We had to trust that God had it under control. We also knew that social services are always more than happy to waive obstacles if it fits their immediate needs. So, we committed to acting in the belief that no form construed by a local social service agency could derail God's plans. Mandy and I believed and affirmed that if God had a child over the age of two in mind for us, He would figure it out.

From the Family Archives (September 2008)

It's been a while since we wrote so we thought we would update you all. As of last week, our paperwork for both our foster license and our adoption home study are officially completed. It has been a long time, but things are winding down. Right now, a file describing our family and home is sitting on the desk of one or more "matchers" who have the responsibility of finding a suitable home when a child becomes available. This also means that any day we could get a call telling us that a child is ready for us to meet. A day or so after the call we'll meet our child and make a decision of yes or no regarding placement. If the answer is yes, then we will have our son or daughter in our home in a matter of days. We'll keep you posted, but it looks like things are coming full circle and we couldn't be more excited. God Bless.

Fast forward a few months. By mid-September 2008, we had finished our homestudy and were ready to be matched with a prospective placement. On September 29, 2008, Mandy received a phone call from our adoption worker. After exchanging a few pleasantries, the caseworker uttered a line that would forever change our lives.

"I know that you are only licensed for children birth to two. However, we have a child we are hoping to match who is three and a half. We think she would be perfect for your family."

Even as I write this eleven years later, I cannot help but smile, and triumphantly proclaim, "Take that world!" No one can out-big God. In case we needed more evidence, that phone call was a not-so-gentle reminder that we were right where God wanted us. Even though bureaucracies and bureaucrats made the road difficult, but God is bigger than our obstacles.

During the phone call, Mandy was provided a little information: the child has developmental issues, the child has behavioral issues; the child has been in nine placements. Then we were asked the big question. "Would you be willing to come down Friday to hear the presentation?" How do you say "no" to this?

"Of course," Mandy replied.

Friday morning, October 3, 2008, we met our caseworker and Summer's (for it was here we learned her name) social worker. A presentation is a formal reading of a court-prepared report of family history, child's history, and placement issues and needs. These are often done on Fridays, so the potential family has the weekend to talk amongst themselves in order to determine if they wish to pursue placement. We were asked to call the following Monday morning and inform the team of our decision to either move forward or to wait until another child was presented.

Following the meeting, Mandy and I got back in our car and looked at each other. "Do we need the weekend?" I asked her.

Tears in her eyes, she looked at me and quietly said, "no."

Again, how could either of us say "no" to God? We knew before we met her, this was right. So, Monday morning, we called Allison and told her we were ready to proceed. That day we were faxed an updated license that allowed us to parent children of all ages-- birth to eighteen.

From the Family Archives (October 6, 2008)

Friday we met with two social workers from within the Orange County social service agency. For the past week, we had been in contact with our social worker regarding a potential candidate for placement. Friday was the formal meeting in which they gave us documentation on development, placement, and history. Prior to Friday, we had only anecdotal reports on these items. We have been asked, following this meeting, whether we wish to pursue a foster/adoption plan with the child we were told about.

We are not sure if this will work out. We don't know how long it will take if it does work out (we're being told that placement steps will take anywhere from 4 to 6 weeks, which is what we expected based on our own professional experience with placement steps). With many questions remaining, we decided to commit to this child. It is a wonderful feeling for Mandy and I to be able to talk to each about a specific child with a specific age and a name. Despite all the roadblocks and obstacles, we are in a better place in this process than we have ever been. We can see how all the steps led to this specific child to this specific moment.

Thursday, October 9th was the day agreed upon to meet Summer for the first time. As we approached the group home, Mandy and I were both nervous. Would she like us? Were we rushing into placing this child? Should we be more circumspect and meet more children? With those questions in our minds, we rang the bell. The house parent and Summer's social worker ushered us inside. Mandy walked in first. In front of her stood the most adorable little girl I had ever seen. Summer extended a hand to Mandy (Apparently, she had been doing a lot of work in her speech and behavioral therapy regarding proper greetings.) and said, "nimeetcha." (aka "nice to meet you") Mandy smiled and said, "hello."

I came in the doorway just after Mandy. I am above average in height (6'4") so when I meet children, I typically get down on one knee so we can be eye to eye. Summer saw me get down on a knee and immediately jumped and took hold of my neck. She took hold of my heart that day. Immediately all doubts disappeared because God is faithful.

Over the next week, we were allowed to visit the house a few times as we got to know each other. On our third visit, the children at the different houses were having a community barbeque. Mandy arrived a bit earlier than and I, so she had time to sit at a picnic table with Summer and some of her housemates. As I entered the backyard, Summer and I made eye contact. Immediately she realized that she was stuck at the picnic table (it was a booth-style picnic table and she was between two adults). So, she crawled under the table, ignoring all the adults' pleas to the contrary. She had one object, me. She ran to me and gave me a hug. She knew that I wasn't there for anybody but her. She knew, at 3 ½, that my whole reason for being in that backyard was her and her alone. These signposts of reassurance were gifts from God. Later, when problems presented themselves, as they were guaranteed to do, it was so easy to look back and remember...God is faithful.

From the Family Archives (October 10, 2008)

Yes, we have met our daughter. Although she is not yet able to live with us, we have had the opportunity to visit her at her residence and get to know her a little. She is more than we could have ever imagined. I never cease to be amazed at the way God chooses to work.

If our adoption process had only taken a couple of months or if our social worker hadn't left us hanging for four months or if. . . or if. . . If things had gone according to our schedule, our process would have looked a lot different. Despite the fact that our daughter (it's just really cool saying that) has been in the system for a considerable period of time we wouldn't have been matched with her at any other time in our adoption process. For reasons I cannot really go into, she was available at just the right time that we authorized. We couldn't be happier.

When our social worker first called us she let us know that a girl might be available, but she warned us that she was not within the age range we requested. Apparently, God knew what we wanted and needed more than we did. We couldn't be happier.

Our social worker explained some of the developmental issues, background, family, social and legal issues surrounding the case to Mandy. I'm sure they give the perceived negatives upfront to sift the prospective parents, but it didn't matter to us. Our social worker also told Mandy about her age, which would require us to get re-licensed to accept her into our home. I'm sure Mandy's response surprised the social worker. Mandy took all the information in and told the social worker, "she sounds perfect."

We have had the chance over the past couple of weeks to get to know this beautiful little girl. Yes, there will be struggles. Yes, there will be frustrations. Yes, the difficulties of the process are not over. We will still have to navigate the system until they give us legal authority, at least six months from now. Yet, she fits perfectly into our family. God, in His wisdom, prepared our home and our hearts and knew 3 1/2 years ago that this wonderful girl would one day end up with us. In the Spring of 2005, we weren't even sure that we would adopt. Even when we thought about adoption, we had no clue how. There were so many unknowns at that time, yet God knew this girl born, not fifteen-minutes from our home, would one day be part of our family.

In a world of economic, political and social uncertainty it is always good to be reminded that the things of God are not left to chance.

After a few visits to the home, they allowed us to take Summer out for a two-hour outing. We had met her on a Thursday (October 9) and this was only the following Friday (October 17). So, two hours was all they gave us, and frankly, all we were ready for.

It was October, and we only had a two-hour pass, so we took Summer to a local pumpkin patch. When we got in the car, she was excited and seemed ready to go. Once we got out of the car at the Pumpkin Patch things changed. At the Pumpkin Patch, she threw tantrum after tantrum. She rolled around the hay-strewn ground yelling and crying. We tried to hold her. To comfort her. To reassure her. Nothing worked as she pushed and fought us. Other visitors looked on in interest and judgment. I am sure they were thinking we were terrible parents, or that she was a terrible child. We were struggling to both keep her safe and to calm her. Yet, we could feel the weight of judgment from the onlookers. This was our first experience, as parents, of what many parents and caregivers of children (and adults) with disabilities experience regularly.

In our defense, this was only our first day being parents. We had not developed, as most parents do, as our child developed. Rather, as foster parents, we were thrust into Summer's life at a particular stage in her development and expected to know her moods and triggers. We were expected to know her cries for help. We were expected to know what she was communicating, even though she did not always have the words. The truth is, we didn't. Well, we managed to get through the afternoon and safely bring her back to the group home.

Afterward, we sat in our car, looked at each other and both said, "are we sure?" It was that difficult, but God chose to step in and give us a gift.

That little comma, the word "but," and the presence of God are the story of our lives. Death—and sickness and disappointment and weariness and betrayal—and the troubles of life all seek to hem us in and bring us low. . .

> "**But God**, being rich in mercy, because of His great love with which He loved us, even when we were dead in our transgressions, made us alive together with Christ" (Ephesians 2:4, ESV).

This is what Paul is trying to explain when he informs the Romans that they can rejoice when hemmed in with troubles. He then admonishes them to stay alert for what God will do next. "In alert expectancy such as this, we're never left feeling short-changed. Quite the contrary—we can't round up enough containers to hold everything God generously pours into our lives through the Holy Spirit!" (Romans 5:3-5, MSG) Time and time again as we journeyed through foster care, through adoption, through disability, through cancer, or through the drudgery of the commonplace, we saw God do more than we had expected.

The world of disability and special education can feel overwhelming. Navigating the child welfare system can feel overwhelming. Receiving a diagnosis of cancer can feel overwhelming. In fact, depending on our context and situation, many, many things can overwhelm us. Yet, scripture reminds us that "Can anything ever separate us from Christ's love? Does it mean he no longer loves us if we have trouble or calamity, or are persecuted, or hungry, or destitute, or in danger, or threatened with death? No, despite all these things, **overwhelming victory** is ours through Christ, who loved us." (Romans 8:35 &37, NLT)

A clarification, I feel, is in order. Note that Paul reminds the Romans that trouble, calamity, persecution, hunger, danger, destitution, and death are part of our sojourn here on earth. **Overwhelming victory** is ours **in** and **through** these things, not **from** these things.

When we feel forgotten and overwhelmed by the floods of life. . .

But God remembered Noah and all the wild animals and the livestock that were with him in the ark, and he sent a wind over the earth, and the waters receded. (Genesis 8:1, NIV)

When weariness sets in, and life is too much to take. . .

- *If the God of my father, the God of Abraham and the Fear of Isaac, had not been with me, you would surely have sent me away empty-handed. **But God** has seen my hardship and the toil of my hands, and last night he rebuked you.* (Genesis 31:42, NIV)

When our enemies are upon us and the snares and traps are set for us. . .

- *You intended to harm me, **but God** intended it for good to accomplish what is now being done, the saving of many lives.* (Genesis 50:20, NIV)
- *David stayed in the desert strongholds and in the hills of the Desert of Ziph. Day after day Saul searched for him, **but God** did not give David into his hands.* (1 Samuel 23:14, NIV)

When I refuse to listen to the word of God. When I walk away time and time again. . .

- *They refused to listen and failed to remember the miracles you performed among them. They became stiff-necked and in their rebellion appointed a leader in order to return to their slavery. **But you are a*** *forgiving God*, *gracious and compassionate, slow to anger and abounding in love. Therefore, you did not desert them.* (Nehemiah 9:17, NIV)

When I feel that God cannot use me, or my story. . .

- *But God chose the foolish things of the world to shame the wise; God chose the weak things of the world to shame the strong.* (1 Corinthians 1:27, NIV)

When life seems hopeless. . .

- *But God will redeem my life from the grave; he will surely take me to himself.* (Psalm 49:15, NIV)
- *My flesh and my heart may fail,* **but God** *is the strength of my heart and my portion forever.* (Psalm 73:26, NIV)

When my situation looks impossible. . .

- *Jesus looked at them and said, "With man this is impossible,* **but with God** *all things are possible.* (Matthew 19:26, NIV)

When I feel unworthy of the love of God or that I am beyond God's love. . .

- *But God demonstrates his own love for us in this: While we were still sinners, Christ died for us.* (Romans 5:8, NIV)

On my own, my story is tragic. On my own, my story is of not much worth. On my own, I would stay lost. On my own, I do not measure up...but God.

Throughout our journey with Summer, we have learned (and truthfully, had to be reminded many times over) that God is bigger than our circumstances. We ran up against the bureaucracy of the child-welfare system, but God made a way. We doubted our ability to parent a child who had been through as much as Summer had, but God sent reminders of His love. We doubted, at times if we were where we needed to be, but God sent signposts to let us know He was in control.

Christian author, blogger, and speaker, Lisa Terkeurst, has a message entitled, "How big is your but?" In it she reminds her readers/listeners of the following:

"I've found a big defeater in my life is following up statements about what I want or need to do with the words 'But I.'

I need to work out... BUT I am so tired.

I want to get healthy... BUT I lack self-control.

I want to stop yelling at my kids... BUT I just feel so frustrated all the time.

I need to talk about this issue with my friend... BUT I don't like confrontation.

When we follow up statements with 'But I' the BUT seems very big.

That's why I'm learning to follow every "but I" with a "But God" statement of truth. If I catch myself saying 'but I'... I need to see this as a trigger to redirect my discouraged heart with a 'But God' truth.

When we follow up statements with 'But God' the BUT becomes smaller and smaller.[7]*"*

This is something I am learning and have been learning since the day God brought our daughter into our lives.

---

[7] Terkeurst, L. (2012). "But God." https://lysaterkeurst.com/2012/02/but-god-verses/

When the way seems hopeless, but God. . .: Now What?

"In the dark night of the soul, bright flows the river of God." St. John of the Cross[8]

There is loss. There are dark nights of the soul. But God. . .

Ann Voskamp opens her New York Times bestseller, *One Thousand Gifts*, by offering her reader a glimpse into her own story[9]. Voskamp tells of the loss of her sister Aimee. She tells of being scarred. Throughout the book, more scars and secrets are revealed. These scars prompt Voskamp to ask the deep-seated questions that those who have made a home in loss and pain often echo. She writes, "[c]an there be a good God? A God who graces with good gifts when a crib lies empty through long nights, and bugs burrow through coffins? Where is God, really?" Here is the question that many have asked as we struggle with scars, both secret and known.

She continues her questioning by giving voice to the doubts and struggles of so many others. "Where," she asks, "hides this joy of the Lord, this God who wills the earth with good things, and how do

---

[8] Saint John of the Cross. (2007). *Dark Night of the Soul: And Other Great Works.* Bridge Logos Foundation.
[9] Voskamp, A. (2010). *One Thousand Gifts: A Dare to Live Fully Right Where You Are.* Zondervan. Grand Rapids, MI.

I fully live when life is full of hurt? How do I wake up to the joy and grace and beauty and all that is the fullest life when I must stay numb to losses and crushed dreams and all that empties me out?"

The way seems hopeless, but God has promised hope. The way seems overwhelming, but God has promised overwhelming victory. The way seems impossible, but all things are possible through God. Yet, *knowing* what the Bible says and *trusting* God's promises toward me are not the same. In fact, trust, real trust, is something much deeper than a head-knowledge of God's promises or table-side collection of aphorisms. Voskamp writes, "I've got to get this thing, what it means to trust, to gut-believe in the good touch of God toward me, because it's true: I can't fill with joy until I learn how to trust."

What exactly does that mean for the believer living in the stress and anxiety, living in the loss and pain, or living in the fear and uncertainty? As I read through Voskamp's beautifully written prose, I am struck by two choices that must be made in those times. The first choice is to *trust,* and the second is to *count.*

TRUST

Trust is a choice. It is not enough to simply *feel* trusting. Rather, I must act in that trust. Voskamp asks, "How can I trust when a troubled, joy-shriveled heart has pumped fear through the stiff veins of all my years?" Simply and directly she answers her own query:" "If I believe, then I must let go and trust."

When the fears of life. The anxieties and stresses of life lie and tell us that God is not trustworthy. They tell us that we must cling to our comforts. They tell us that the current troubles have no purpose, that God will not deliver, and that the way is hopeless.

Trust says otherwise. Trust leans into God's character. Trust calls us to stop being a loss-tourist and to build a home alongside the broken. Trust is pursuing foster care and adoption when it is scary. Too often, I have had well-meaning friends let me know that foster care or adoption has "been on their heart" yet it wasn't "the right time." Trust informs us that God's time to build a home, to take up residence, is right now.

If you are on the fence now is the time to trust. Extend grace to the family impacted by disability. Go to that information meeting on foster care. Fill out the application for adoption. Move out of fear and into hope by purposefully and actively trusting. For the act of trusting is an act of belief that God is in fact bigger than. . .it all. In choosing trust Voskamp articulates a truth that is both true and uncomfortable. She writes, "If authentic, saving belief is the act of trusting, then to choose stress is an act of disbelief. . .atheism."

COUNT

How do I trust when my life is a mess? How do I lean into God's promises when I don't see them? It is difficult. For many, it is difficult to embrace their local church when pastor after pastor tells them that their child would be better off "somewhere else." It is difficult to trust when there are no scars, simply because there are still open wounds from loss, abuse, disappointment, broken dreams and broken hearts. Voskamp asks simply, "How do you count on life when the hopes don't add up?" Yet, within that question lies the answer she has found to be true, "Count blessings and discover who can be counted on."

When I look back through scripture, I see a string of hopeless encounters. Yet, in the midst, I see a God who comes through. I see a God that reminds His people of how He comes through. Time and time again, God retells the story of His providence. When the children of Israel are afraid and unwilling to remember, God recounts His faithfulness.

So, what do I do when the way seems hopeless? I count. I remember. I seek the small favors of a great God. I remind myself of God's provision, which emboldens me to actively trust.

Voskamp compares God's faithfulness to a sturdy stone bridge. Time and again she crosses that bridge, but too often she fails to be thankful for the builder who put that piece of grace into her world. If God is the great bridge builder than "I'm grateful to the Bridge Builder for the crossing of a million strong bridges," she writes, "thankful for a million faithful moments, my life speaks my belief and I trust Him again."

It is not always easy to count my blessings when the way seems hopeless. Yet, choose to do so. When I cannot do that, I ask for help. I ask those I love to speak blessing into my life. When I see others in the same despair, I choose to speak blessing into their lives. Mind you, I do not preach, but rather, I choose to be a blessing and to count blessings alongside them, even while I build a home in their pain and loss. This is faith. "Anything less than gratitude and trust, Voskam cautions, "is practical atheism."

Lesson #3: We were made to belong

There is a scene in the Disney movie, The Greatest Game Ever Played, in which the character of Francis Ouimette (played by Shia Labouef), a golf caddy with dreams of winning the 1913 U.S. Open, is at a pre-tournament party. At this party, a member of the exclusive golf club where Ouimette caddies, approaches young Francis with disdain, and says, "Young man, you may have been invited, but don't get the idea that you belong[10]." The point the club member is making is that inclusion (at the party in this case) and belonging are fundamentally different concepts. Individuals who forget the difference should, according to this club member, be reminded. This distinction between being included in the invitation list and belonging at the party is, apparently, lost in the larger discourse of those involved in disability ministry. This is of relevance as the modern American Christian Church has increasingly been compared to an actual country club. Theologian John Swinton argues that inclusion is primarily a political concept designed to ensure basic rights. Yet, this political concept is void of an "innate moral mechanism within the contemporary political discourse that might obligate or even encourage people to love those whom society considers different." Yet, we all desire a place of belonging.

---

[10] Blocker, D., Brezner, L., Frost, M., Steinberg, D. (Producer), & Paxton, B. (Director). (2005). *The Greatest Game Ever Played* [Motion picture]. United States: Disney.

From the Family Archives (October 22, 2008)

We are excited and delighted to be able to get to know our daughter. Our visits with her have been going exceptionally well. Anytime a child has had multiple placements, social workers are concerned about the transition process. As a result, we have slowly worked our way into her life. As professionals in the field, we completely understand the social worker's need to protect her client from too much disruption. As parents, we cannot get her into our home fast enough.

I will never forget the first day I met her. Her social worker and her house parent walked her over to where I was kneeling and said, "say 'hi' to Mike." She looked at me, smiled and jumped into my arms. This was more than I hoped for. As we were leaving the visit that day, I had her in my arms and told her that I had to go. She looked at her worker and said, "bye" thinking she was going with me. Mandy and I would have taken her home that day if we could, but we understand the process. However, understanding the process does not make things easier.

For the past couple of weeks, Mandy and I have visited with her four days a week. Every night (whether we are visiting her group home or spending the day at our home and then going to her group home) we help her get ready for bed. Mandy helps her with a bath, we tuck her in, read with her, pray with her, sing with her and give her goodnight kisses. Our prayer is the same each night. We thank God for her, and we pray that those who get the opportunity to see her in the morning take good care of her.

We don't yet get to be the people who wake her up. The days we don't get to see her are torture. Someone else is doing the job we want to do. Someone else is starting her day. After having her visit this past weekend, our house seems quiet and lonely without her. We know that this will soon be a memory, but the waiting is the hard part. Saying "goodnight" hurts and not seeing her for days at a time hurts. Yet, we know that this will pass.

This brief time has also taught us compassion for other parents. We know there are plenty of parents who, for one reason or another, have to live with fractured time with their child. Maybe your child lives in a facility, hospital or other institution. Perhaps your child is splitting time between two parents. We don't know what the reason is, but our little experience (which in the light of a lifetime, is extremely short) has led us to think of you all in our prayers and pray that God will bring you comfort when you are parted.

The week after our disastrous outing with Summer, we were permitted to allow her to spend the night with us. We were nervous. This was completely new to us. This was far removed from babysitting a niece or nephew. We were now in the realm of parental responsibility. So, Friday, October 24, we picked Summer up from her group home and brought her to our little apartment. Summer remembered her visit the weekend prior and made a beeline for her bedroom. We spent the evening playing games, watching movies, and having fun together. As that first night ended, we tucked her into her bed. Mandy read her a story, and I prayed over her. I prayed that night that she would, as time went by, come to expect and demand. I put my hand on her hands and prayed, "Dear Lord, thank you for Summer. Thank you that she is in our life. Thank you that we get to be her mommy and daddy. Help us to be a good mommy and daddy for her." It has been over twelve years since that first night, and I still pray that prayer nightly.

After Summer went to sleep, Mandy and I stayed up, nervous and excited. We talked for hours about how we were feeling. We remembered the embarrassment and frustration from the week prior. Our conversation began to drift into the obstacles in our path. We talked about the system, about Summer's history, about our families, about Summer's diagnoses, and about how woefully unprepared we were to take on the responsibility of navigating all "this."

Saturday morning came early. Neither Mandy nor I are early risers, so Summer had the advantage on us. Summer woke early and snuck into our bedroom. She then proceeded to crawl quietly under the blankets until she was laying between Mandy and I. Mandy and I looked at each other and smiled. We were both thinking that this was fun, or this was cute. Yet, Summer made it something more. She reached one hand under Mandy's neck and another hand under my neck. She then pulled our heads together, so that we were all cheek-to-cheek. Rolling our heads back and forth, and with all the joy she could muster and said, "family."

That single moment has stayed in the forefront of our hearts ever since. Summer reminded us that we weren't the only ones pursuing a family. She reminded us that God was in this process. Summer reminded us that she too was on a journey. We could complain about the bureaucracy of social services. We could dwell on how unprepared we felt. We could question whether this was going to work out. Yet, meanwhile, Summer was in desperate need of a family. She was in desperate need of belonging. And she had chosen us.

From the Family Archives (November 10, 2008)

It has been one month since the first time Mandy and I met our, then, daughter-to-be and only ten days since she was placed in our home. However, there are times when we feel like she has always been ours. In fact, it is difficult to remember life when she was not part of it. Now I am not saying that everything is sunshine and roses. We have had some difficult moments, but that is to be expected due to a variety of environmental and development needs in her life. Yet, the beautiful experiences far outweigh any difficulty. Every night after Mandy and I have tucked her into bed, we sit down and just talk about how blessed we are to have been given this gift. Even though our daughter is a gift in her own right, the true gift she brings into our life is the gift of family.

Children need family. This seems obvious, but many people just do not get it. A child, such as our daughter, needs a mother and father. Research clearly indicates the truth of this. The outcomes of children who grow up in foster care demonstrate the truth of this. I could cite stats on how divorce, child abuse, infidelity, and other family-breakers lead to negative outcomes, but I do not need that.

My beautiful daughter spent the first 3+ years of her life without a family. Despite this, she seems to indicate an innate need for family. In her short life, she has never had a "daddy." She has never referred to another man as "daddy." We have been told that she is affectionate, and that she has consistently given hugs and kisses to those near her, and that makes us sad. It saddens us because we are pretty sure that she has never had someone tuck her in at night and say prayers, or worse, say "I love you." These are all integral to being a family.

Since we have known our little girl, she has repeatedly referred to Mandy as "mommy." As she learns more words and signs, she is eager to show them or say them to her "mommy." The other night she threw her arms around my neck and said, "my daddy!" Now she repeatedly refers to both Mandy and me as "mommy and daddy." Why? Mandy and I believe that more than anything our daughter has been eager for family. She has had a tough time and tough early life so far, but despite all of that she responds when we tell her we love her.

This is what amazes Mandy and me. We look at our little girl and are amazed that she can be so full of love when her life has been so devoid of it for so long. She is a miracle to us. Both of us are more convinced that God loves us today than we were one month ago. We cannot begin to understand the graciousness of God that brought her to our lives. Yet, we do know that God is a God who loves family and we are thankful for that.

Remember those three stories Jesus told about loss? Let's revisit those for a few minutes. When the Pharisees chastise Jesus at the beginning of chapter fifteen of Luke's gospel, they are not asking why Jesus is eating with sinners. They "muttered" that "This man welcomes sinners and eats with them." (Luke 15:2, NIV). It scandalizes them that Jesus would "welcome" (the KJV uses the term "receiveth" instead of "welcome" which, I think, rolls off the tongue quite nicely) sinners *AND* eat with them. It is no longer just the eating, but also the welcome Jesus provides that is scandalous.

In response to the critique of welcome, Jesus tells three stories about *welcome*, belonging, and love as well as the interconnectedness of each of these. In the first story, Jesus relates the tale of the lost sheep. In John 10:11-15, Jesus informs His listeners He is the good shepherd. Being a good shepherd, He knows His sheep. When one of those sheep goes missing, then they are missed. They are missed because they are known by the shepherd. Every one of the sheep belongs to the shepherd, not because of what they contribute to the shepherd, but because of who the shepherd is and the value they hold because they are His.

In the same manner, Jesus tells another story about belonging. This time the something missing is a few measly coins. A few coins can be discarded or deemed worthless. Yet, when they are gone, they are missed because the woman knows the value of all she has. So, if anything is lost, she knows. Because she knows what is lost, the house is scoured and searched in order to find what was lost. Just like the found sheep in the first parable, the woman celebrates the return of what was lost. Being missed is essential to these stories. It is essential to belonging, as is the celebration.

In the telling of these stories, Jesus is reminding his listeners (e.g. the Pharisees) that the welcoming He is being chastised for is essential to our understanding of what love is. He reinforces this point in the story of the prodigal son. This story demonstrates that the love of the father creates welcome. This is true regardless of what the son has done. Yet, in his deep yearnings, the son also longs to belong.

When Summer came to us, she was yearning to belong. Mandy and I were yearning to belong as well. As a child living and moving through the child welfare system and as a child labeled with disabilities, Summer has (and continues to) struggled with finding a place to belong. Yet, she was made to belong. I believe that when true belonging takes place, there is, and there should be, as Jesus describes in all three stories, much rejoicing.

There are a lot of well-intentioned programs out there designed to support children in care. Yet make no mistake, children in care do not need a week vacation or a birthday party or a computer or school supplies. None of these are bad in and of themselves, but they can be distractions from the thing that all children need...families. Family is a God-designed institution. Summer instinctively knew this. Summer had about twenty-five words when she came to live with us. Summer had never known family in a true sense. Yet, Summer knew what she was missing, and she knew what she had found. And as all three stories suggest, there was much rejoicing when the three of us found each other.

I wish I could say that Summer has always found a place of belonging. Sadly, this has not always been the case. Two stories illustrate this well.

Just like Francis Ouimette's character from "The Greatest Game Ever Played," Summer (and by extension Mandy and I) has experienced inclusion without belonging, specifically in our relationship with our local churches. So, what is the difference? The ubiquitous use of the word "inclusion," particularly within churches and similarly situated faith-communities gives the impression that the belonging found in Luke 15 and the inclusion espoused by many local churches are the same. Unfortunately, too often, particularly with individuals impacted by disability, there is a tendency toward inclusion without belonging.

Theologian John Swinton in an interview on the difference between belonging and inclusion points out that "The idea of belonging, then, is a lot richer and more theological [than inclusion]." He explains that "It means that you are in the room but also you belong in the room." He continues to identify the heart of this difference by saying, "you know that you belong when you're missed." He concludes that "It's that kind of deep longing and that deep missing that is the essence of the body of Christ."

For us, we have learned that true belonging is premised on the fact that both parties can, and do, regularly choose one another both by their actions and shared presence. Whereas inclusion is too often approached as something one party chooses to offer or impose upon another. As a result, we have been in too many rooms where we were "technically" included but were not too subtly shown that we did not belong. Unfortunately, this is something too many families impacted by disability know full well. At three different churches, we were told that Summer would be included in the Children's, Junior High School, or High School ministries if either Mandy or I sat with her and kept her from distracting the other students. In other words, we were sent a direct message that she did not belong in the ministry, that no room or attempt to make her belong would be made as it was just too much work. Summer could watch, she could observe, but she could not contribute or belong. Other families feel this same inclusion/belonging challenge within their families, communities, or friend-groups. Yet the move to belonging should not be construed to be so difficult as to prevent real welcome.

How does a church move from inclusion to belonging? For belonging to occur, a church must extend welcome by sending the message that everyone is loved, is wanted, has a purpose, and is missed when they are absent.

YOU ARE LOVED

While inclusion is a necessary step within church communities, it is not the primary call or purpose. Again, John Swinton, author of *Becoming Friends of Time: Disability, Timefullness, and Gentle Discipleship*, points out that "[i]t is the ability to love, not the ability to include or tolerate, that is the primary mark of discipleship." The welcome that leads to belonging must begin and end with love. "For," Swinton continues, "[t]he vocation of the Christian community is to learn to love God, and in coming to love God, learn what it means to love and to receive love from all of its members[11]."

---

[11] Swinton, J. (2017). *Becoming Friends of Time: Disability, Timefullness, and Gentle Discipleship.* Baylor University Press.

In perhaps the most famous passage on love, the Apostle Paul offers a model of love that transcends ability or perceived disability and labels as he states:

"If I speak in the tongues of men or of angels, but do not have love, I am only a resounding gong or a clanging cymbal. If I have the gift of prophecy and can fathom all mysteries and all knowledge, and if I have a faith that can move mountains, but do not have love, I am nothing. If I give all I possess to the poor and give over my body to hardship that I may boast, but do not have love, I gain nothing (I Cor. 13: 1-3 NIV)."

When the local body prioritizes knowledge, ability, wealth, or anything beyond love and loving, it is in direct opposition to a Biblical model of welcome that leads to belonging. Therefore, love must be embedded in all welcome for belonging to occur.

Like the Prodigal Son, I know that I am loved when the father wraps me in His arms and lets me know that I am loved. Summer, despite the challenges she has faced, wraps me in her love and lets me know that we belong together.

YOU ARE WANTED

It is one thing to be included, yet it is something else entirely to be wanted. The pull to be wanted, to be involved, and to connect transcends ability. We demonstrate that another is wanted by creating space, both physically and temporally, for that individual. Therefore, the fact that many local churches implicitly argue that all individuals are wanted as long as they fit into the schedule or assigned space, creates major barriers to belonging, something we have experienced in profoundly hurtful ways.

In the stories of Zacchaeus (Luke 19-1:10) and the woman at the well (John 4:4-26) Jesus demonstrates how to communicate a desire for belonging. Jesus explicitly creates a space in which to invite the other into a belonging far better than they are currently experiencing. The belonging Jesus offers is squarely balanced on the fact that the individuals Jesus calls are wanted, that communion is wanted, and that fellowship is wanted. Perhaps most telling, the belonging Jesus offers does so in full awareness that they are wanted because of who Jesus is, not because of what Zacchaeus or the Woman at the Well have to offer in return. A church that reaches out and demonstrates a desire for fellowship, without condition, embodies the belonging seen in the Gospel.

YOU HAVE A PURPOSE HERE

The Church is a congregation, or community, of disciples, as such recognizing that ALL members, regardless of perceived ability, have the opportunity to discover their purpose as disciples of Christ is a necessary step on the road to belonging. In "Rethinking Evangelism," Dallas Willard defines discipleship as:

"a person who has decided that the most important thing in their life is to learn how to do what Jesus said to do. A disciple is not a person who things under control or knows a lot of things. Disciples simply are people

who are constantly revising their affairs to carry through on their decision to follow Jesus." [12]

Put this way, the intellectual markers often used to identify disciples are unnecessary and can lead to isolation. Therefore, Swinton reminds us that to be "implicitly or explicitly perceived as a non-disciple within the 'community of disciples' leads to a lack of belonging which stems from a lack of perceived purpose."

It is, therefore, incumbent upon local churches to take seriously the call "to go and make disciples of all nations, baptizing them in the name of the Father and of the Son and of the Holy Spirit (Matthew 28:19)." Note the lack of qualifiers in the "ALL" of this commission. Which begs the question, how is the local church demonstrating to all that everyone has a purpose and a calling with the body?

Summer asked me once, "Daddy, what is it that people know is special about me?"

I did not really understand the question, so she continued. "Is it that I make people feel welcomed?"

"Yes," I replied. "Summer of all the gifts God has given you, one for sure is that you make people feel loved and feel welcomed." If this is part of her God-ordained purpose, then my responsibility as a father is to help her live that out. My daughter is here for a purpose. God has given her meaning and purpose. As she pursues God, I passionately desire that she live her purpose. It humbles me to think that very thing might be mine.

---

[12] Willard, D. (2001). "Rethinking Evangelism." Retrieved from Dallas Willard website: http://www. dwillard. org/articles/artview. asp.

YOU ARE MISSED WHEN YOU ARE NOT HERE

Belonging, or at least a sense of belonging, is premised on the idea that an individual is missed when they are absent. Moreover, the idea of being missed is not merely a feeling of absence, but rather an active pursuit of those who are missed. In the above, Swinton references the "essence of the body of Christ." Paul states in I Corinthians 12:12 (NIV) that "Just as a body, though one, has many parts, but all its many parts form one body, so it is with Christ." If this is true, then how can local faith communities do anything but seek the missing pieces of their bodies?

We had been going to a church in South Orange County for a few years when there was a change in Junior High leadership. The new approach and style of the new Jr. High Director resulted in a tough environment for Summer to fit in. Since Mandy worked in the nursery during services, Summer and I hung out in the lobby during service. Prior to resigning ourselves to the lobby, Mandy and I had met with the Jr. High director to see how Summer could become involved. We, of course, were met with the typical question, "Can one of you stay with her?" This, as I mentioned before, is tantamount to saying that Summer does not belong, nor will the ministry make room for her. We then approached the church leadership (pastor and associate). We had a productive meeting with the leadership and attempted to problem-solve pathways to Summer being integrated into the Jr High Ministry.

For nearly nine months, Summer and I sat in the church lobby every Sunday morning. For nearly nine months we reached out to church leadership, including the Jr. High pastor. Yet, despite being a small church with a Jr. High/Middle School attendance of less than two dozen students, no one ever said, "Summer, we miss you." They did not say it by action or by language. As a result, we left that community. Why? We (not just Summer) did not belong. My daughter is part of me, as is my wife and my son. If one does not belong, we do not belong. Ultimately, it's the idea that we weren't missed. Neither Summer's contributions (of which there are many), nor Summer's gifts (which are obvious to most), nor Summer's heart (which is kind and good) were ever really welcomed, and therefore never missed.

Nearly twenty-five years ago a theology professor gave me a book written by Jean Vanier, founder of L'Arche communities, titled *Community and Growth*. L'Arche communities are residential communities of welcome, designed specifically for individuals labeled with intellectual disabilities. In this book, Vanier outlined the history of L'Arche communities. In his chronicle of the development and growth of the organization, Vanier noted that "If that thirst to belong and be in communion with another is not satisfied, the pain and anguish rises up and with it feelings of guilt, anger, and hate." What would be better than guilt, anger, and hate? I think the late Jean Vanier would argue that love, belonging, and welcome—the welcome embodied in Christ would be better? [13]

---

[13] Jean Vanier passed away in 2019. In 2020 l'Arche revealed that Vanier was guilty of sexual misconduct. Even now I struggle to reconcile the writing and work of Vanier that inspired me with the antithesis of those standards as they came to light in February 2020. I am not sure I know what to make of it all. I know I cannot simply discard the truths that were dispensed, but I am not sure what to do with the rest.

We were made to belong: Now What?

"Christianity is not about learning how to live within the lines; Christianity is about the joy of coloring." – Mike Yaconelli, Dangerous Wonder[14].

When I was in college, a friend of mine introduced me to a character that would have an immense influence on my thinking and believing by the name of Mike Yaconelli. I first encountered Mike through his writing within the *Wittenberg Door*, which let me know that my own thoughts on "church culture" had a place they belonged. Later, I learned about an organization designed to support individuals as they sought to create spaces of belonging for youth within the local church, known as Youth Specialties. I would later learn more about Mike. I would learn about his heart for l'Arche communities, a community that has shaped my journey. I would learn about his story and his unique voice and contribution to a church culture rife with the legalism of my youth.

Yet, I also began learning about welcome and belonging, through a small, straightforward book called *Messy Spirituality*, with the spot-on subtitle of *God's Annoying Love for Imperfect People*[15]. A

---

[14] Yaconelli, M. (2014). *Dangerous Wonder: The Adventure of Childlike Faith.* Tyndale House.
[15] Yaconelli, M. (2007). *Messy spirituality: God's Annoying Love for Imperfect People* Harper Collins.

lesson that would find its clarity embodied in the life of my amazing daughter.

As I read through this wonderful text, I am reminded of what I must do to live out the truth that we all were made to belong. The lesson I learned from Summer was that we were made to belong. I recognized that belonging and welcome convey a message that one is loved, wanted, has purpose, and is missed when not present. While I believe that to be true, it begs the question of how. How do I live this forward?

Many of the religious leaders of today have the same problem as the religious leaders during the time of Christ. They had an idea of what a Messiah was supposed to look like. He was supposed to be comfortable with the powerful and privileged. He was supposed to favor and reinforce the existing social structures. As such, He was supposed to keep out those who made the establishment feel uncomfortable, what Mike Yaconelli refers to as the "riff-raff." Today, the riff-raff in the modern American suburban church are individuals with disabilities, the poor, the homeless, the immigrant, the non-English speaker, and the list seems to grow and grow and grow.

The religious leaders, then and now, had a script in mind for what a Messiah was supposed to look like. I thoroughly enjoy the way that Mike Yaconelli frames this idea. He writes, "When Jesus announced he was the Messiah, the Pharisees and others screamed at him, 'There is no Jesus in the Messiah script. Messiahs do not hang out with losers. . . Our Messiah does not disregard his reputation, befriend riffraff, or frequent the haunts of questionable people'." So far, this seems a clear indictment of religious leaders of our own time. Yet, Mike doesn't end it there. Rather, he imagines a response from a Savior that loves the riff-raff beyond anything we might presume to be reasonable. He imagines Jesus' reply, "This Messiah does!" I have read that section in Mike's book on many occasions. I have both cried and laughed. I have never been unmoved. But what do I do with this?

I ACCEPT CHRIST'S WELCOME

The welcome Christ provides is embodied in those three parables of lost sheep, lost coins, and a lost son. The pursuit of the lost and the subsequent rejoicing upon their return is the welcome Jesus offers. Jesus says, "Come to me, all you who are weary and burdened, and I will give you rest." (Matt 11:28, NIV) How amazing is that? Yet, we often miss the point. We forget that Jesus' call was to ALL. We mistakenly think we must be something else before He will welcome us. We forget that the crowds that followed Jesus, the individuals who loved Home, and the disciples that would go on to change the world, were initially a mess. The early followers of Jesus were not the neat and proper Pharisees. They were the outcasts trying to look in, they were the ones who found their lives wrecked and sinking, the ones whose attempts to color inside the lines were made with the fierce reprimands of their failures.

Yet, Jesus offered to remind them not of the need to color inside the lines. Rather He reminded them, as Mike Yaconelli says, "the joy of coloring." If I cannot accept two truths: One, I do not deserve (as neither a lost lamb, a few lost coins, or a rebellious son do) nor have I done anything to warrant the love Jesus offers. And two, Jesus still loves me. He still welcomes me. He still *receiveth* me. This is the heart of what Mike Yaconelli refers to as *Messy Spirituality* which he defines as "the delirious consequence of a life ruined by a

Jesus who will love us right into his arms." Before I can welcome, I must know the welcome of a Jesus who loves me right into His arms.

I EXTEND CHRIST'S WELCOME

If the welcome Jesus offers is available to me, even me. How can I not extend that to others?

If I am to extend Christ's welcome, I must let others know that they are loved. I mean truly loved in a way that is evidenced in both my attitude and my actions. I must let people know that they are not only loved, but wanted, have purpose and are missed. This means that even those that rub me the wrong way. Those that are awkward. Those that bother me. Those that annoy me. Those that seem to be working against my own daughter (within and outside the local church). Yes, all those individuals are welcomed in the family God. I want all of these individuals to be embraced in the arms of our savior's welcome.

Too often, it is easy to forget that we do not deserve to be invited into the family of God. We have not earned our invitation. Yet, we set up rules once we are in that disallows others to enter the fellowship we enjoy. Mike Yaconelli reflects on this attitude within the church by drawing attention to the irony embedded within this approach to fellowship. He writes:

> *Nothing in the church makes people in the church more angry than grace. It's ironic: we stumble into a party we weren't invited to and find the uninvited standing at the door making sure no other uninviteds get in. Then a strange phenomenon occurs: as*

soon as we are included in the party because of Jesus' irresponsible love, we decide to make grace "more responsible" by becoming self-appointed Kingdom Monitors, guarding the kingdom of God, keeping the riff raff out (which, as I understand it, are who the kingdom of God is supposed to include).

I extend welcome by NOT becoming a Kingdom Monitor. I proclaim the Good News when I embrace the truth that Grace is open to all. You can never be too. . .well, anything. I need not stand watch as a gatekeeper. Nor do I need to gatekeep the gatekeepers. I must be busy extending the warm embrace of a Savior who embraced me just as I was/am to those who are in desperate need of that embrace.

So, when a social worker, teacher, parents, church leader, community member, or any other self-appointed gatekeeper informs me that my daughter is too [fill in the blank] or not enough [fill in the blank] to be welcomed in a particular setting, I must doubly embrace welcome. First, I must ensure that my daughter is welcomed. I must, occasionally, fight for her. I must always as Ezekiel says, "stand in the gap" (Ezekiel 22:30) against injustice. Second, I must recognize that those across the table, in the meeting, on the phone, or in the same pew are individuals in new of welcome and I do not have permission to say, "well, since you were such a jerk to me and my kid, you don't belong her in worship with me." No, I must extend the welcome to them as well.

This is something I am still trying to figure out. But even though I fail at this, even though I make a mess of this. I know that my Savior loves me, wants me, has created me with a purpose, and seeks me when I am lost, because I still belong to Him.

Lesson #4: The urgent things are not always the essential things

"Hi, I'm Summer Hoggatt, when I was five, I had kidney cancer," Summer offers as a way of introduction to most new "friends" she meets. (For Summer, anyone she meets is a friend regardless of the setting.)

"Are you OK now?" they ask.

"Yes," she responds with a smile, then continues, "because God was there."

I mentioned previously how Summer's scars are the markers she uses to orient her to God's faithfulness. However, the scar she is most proud of came after she met her forever family. . .

Early on April 21, 2010, just four days after Summer's fifth birthday, I heard Mandy yell for me to get to the bathroom. Summer was sitting in the bathroom and Mandy had her blood-soaked diaper in her hand. Mind you, we did not have a formal history, or at least not an exhaustive one, so Mandy immediately took her to our pediatrician. Our pediatrician quickly determined that it was not a urinary infection and that it required additional expertise. He referred us to Children's Hospital of Orange County, where we met with an Endocrinologist, Dr. Farshid. Over the next several weeks, our doctor met with Summer, did pelvic ultrasound and blood tests (much to the chagrin of Summer). Nothing. No bleeding, but no information from the tests. Just a great dreadful unknown that we were walking into.

Then, about four weeks after the first symptoms, Summer was watching tv with us in our living room and she began to double-over in obvious pain. One problem at this point was that Summer's language was still limited. As such, her ability to help us understand her pain was equally limited. Yet, Summer's diaper was once again soaked in blood. So, we were back in the doctor's office. Our doctor conducted another ultrasound and ran more blood tests. Still no answers. After consulting several colleagues across the country, a tentative diagnosis of *early-onset* or "precocious" puberty was guardedly offered. This diagnosis was followed up in early June with more tests targeted to confirm or disprove the diagnosis. The tests began to wear on all of us. We were in the hospital (since the Dr.'s office was in the hospital) all too regularly.

Yet after another four weeks, Summer was again hunched over in tears because of obvious pain, as once again, we found a blood-soaked diaper. As a result, we were once again in the doctor's office. Our doctor told us she was going to schedule another set of ultrasounds. At that time, Mandy told the doctor that Summer had been favoring her left side. She explained that Summer was shying away from hugs on that side, something Summer never did nor ever does. In fact, there seemed to be a tough bruise around her left midsection. The doctor felt Summer's side and amended the ultrasound order to include her abdomen and chest. The ultrasound was scheduled on mine and Mandy's eighth anniversary, July 19, 2010.

So, Monday morning, July 19th, Mandy and I dutifully took Summer to get her ultrasound. This had become routine for us, so we did not expect much. In fact, we had set up a babysitter so we could have a nice date night. Yet, by the time we got home from the ultrasound, I received a phone call from our doctor. Mind you, this was only about an hour and a half after we completed the ultrasound.

"Mr. Hoggatt, this is Doctor Farshid," she began. "I have the results from Summer's ultrasound from this morning," she continued.

"Yes?" is all I could think to say.

"We found a growth in her midsection, which concerns us," she said. My mind tends to go to some weird places in times of stress, so suddenly, I began to think, "Who is us?" Is this like the royal "we" or am I on speakerphone? Should I ask? I don't ask, of course. I respond with "Ok," waiting for the other shoe to drop. While I do, I nod as though I am absolutely calm and collected as if to say, "Bring it on, I'm strong enough to handle it." The truth was that I was shaking and ready to break. Then, I began wondering, "why am I nodding?" It's not like she can see me."

Then it comes. The moment that, unknown to Summer, would come to shape her identity, arrived. As Dr. Farshid continued, "I have a bed waiting at CHOC on the oncology floor. She needs to be admitted tonight."

I cannot remember what I said next, nor what Dr. Farshid said. I remember walking back into the house (for Mandy and I to get cell reception we had to have phone calls on the porch). As I walked into the house, I remember seeing Mandy and Summer in the sitting on the couch. They were perfect. They were perfectly happy. They were perfectly beautiful. I savored that moment for a brief time. I wanted to enjoy it. I wanted to remember it.

"What did she say?" Mandy eagerly asked, awakening me from my thoughts.

Now I do not claim to be a medical genius, but I knew enough even back then to know that oncology is associated with cancer. So, I looked at my wife and told her that our daughter had cancer. I may have done more difficult things in my life, but I am not sure I have ever given voice to a more difficult thought in my life. So, with fear and trembling, we drove to Children's Hospital of Orange County and checked in.

Upon arrival, we found our room and settled in. Summer was given an IV and we would run a series of tests with her. Around eight in the evening, we were told that Summer would be taken to get her C.T. Scan. So, we followed the nurses and orderlies as they wheeled her bed downstairs into the basement. By ten o'clock we were done and back in our room. That night we slept on the parent "bed." (I say bed euphemistically because it really was just a small chair that folded out into a terrible twin bed, the kind of bed that makes futons seem comfortable). Needless to say, we did not sleep well that night.

So, early the next morning, groggy and a bit disheveled, we met the surgeon. He told us that Summer had an advanced form of cancer and that he would need to operate if she was to survive. He told us that her kidney had to be removed immediately, but that this form of surgery carried its own challenges and potential dangers. With no real choice, we scheduled the surgery for the next morning. The surgery took place early on a Wednesday morning, July 21st.

We would later be informed as to why Summer's body deceived the medical experts. We were told that she must have been in immense pain, though she rarely displayed it. Her entire left kidney had been consumed with a tumor. The tumor was so large that it broke off into her lungs and consumed surrounding tissue. Yet, the effect of the tumor was to disrupt her urinary system, resulting in clotted blood from that kidney being released through the bladder. The problem was that the clotted blood was so thick that it would not easily be released. Apparently, after about four weeks of build up the blood would release, thus the signs. I still marvel at her grace and strength during that time. She still smiled and laughed. She rarely cried. She remained playful and happy despite the pain and discomfort.

It seemed like the morning took forever to arrive. Mandy and I barely slept. We still had the same small green convertible that we had the night before, so the two of us did not have much hope of rest that night. Instead, we spent the night watching Summer sleep. She seemed to sleep peacefully with no fear of the IVs and tubes hooked up to her body, nor with fear of what tomorrow had in store. In fact, around two in the morning, I drove back to our home to gather some belongings, not knowing how long our stay would be, but that is another story.

Early the next morning, the orderlies came to transport Summer to surgery. They wheeled summer from the third-floor Oncology Unit at CHOC to the elevator. The elevator took us down to the basement level, which allowed Summer to be transported under the street next door to St. Joseph's Hospital where the surgery would be performed. During the entire journey, Summer was sitting up smiling and waving at everyone that crossed her path. Meanwhile, Mandy and I vainly attempted to be as upbeat and positive as our little girl.

We finally arrived in the surgical unit where we had to say goodbye to our little girl and place her into the hands of another. As the surgery team approached, she smiled as wide as possible and said, "Hi doctor" as if greeting a friend. Then she peered around the doctor's shoulder to where Mandy and I were standing and, smiling, gave us a wave as if to let us know not to be afraid. That was a significant moment for each of us. There is something inspiring and incouraging when you witness the courage of another.

As we walked into the waiting room, my parents were there, as were two dear friends. I could write pages about both Connie and Amy. Suffice it to say that both have made a life of creating moments of welcome and blessing for individuals too often cast aside. Their presence and that of my parents provided a strength that we sorely needed at that moment. We hugged each member of our team and thanked them for their presence. They encouraged Mandy and me to go get some breakfast while they waited. (never underestimate the importance of people who make you eat when you do not feel like it)

While our friends and family sat in the lobby praying for us, Mandy and I found a little quiet place in the cafeteria to sit with each other. I still vividly recall eating the cafeteria's Wednesday special of Huevos Rancheros. To this day, I cannot order or eat Huevos Rancheros without going, in my mind, back to that morning. I remember giving voice to the fact that Summer had already been through so much in her brief life. She had survived so much. I shook a fist at heaven and wondered why.

By Wednesday afternoon, the surgeon reported that the surgery had been a success. Summer's entire left kidney had been removed. She had also had her port implanted and was quickly returned to her room in the Children's Hospital Oncology unit.

There she would recover now, hooked up to more tubes and needles than before. During that time, we waited. We recognized that the most important thing we could do was simply to wait. To be present. We could not DO anything; we could only wait and be present. Summer needed time and rest. These were the important things she needed. The essential things.

We also needed time to rest and recover. The next two weeks Mandy and I took it in turns as Summer slowly recovered. At times, it was difficult to watch. Summer tended to pull out her tubes, so she had to have elbow splints that prevented her from bending her arms. She hated that. Each time staff from the hospital (orderly, nurse or doctor) entered the room she would immediately begin crying, "doctor doctor, *pleeees*" as she lifted arms hoping that someone would have pity on her and remove the elbow splints. After two weeks of recovery, Summer began both her chemotherapy and her radiation treatments while in the hospital. Yet, within a short while, she was well enough for us to take her home again.

However, before we went home, she was shown a picture of her tumor (it was large enough that research hospitals wanted some). She was so excited to see how large it was that the hospital allowed her to take the photo home. Once home she could not wait to show off her scar that went from her belly button to the middle of her back. She was so proud of that scar and continues to see it as a badge of honor.

While Summer could focus on the cause of her scars, that is not how she sees the world. Rather, she sees her scars as reminders that God did not forget her. Since she was a little girl, Summer would (and still does) get excited whenever she would see a rainbow. "Daddy, look, a rainbow." She would yell excitedly. I would smile at her and ask, "...and what does a rainbow mean." She would smile back and say, "God always keeps His promises."

Now at fifteen years of age, she praises the God who heals. The same God who keeps his promises. Now she compares her scars to His rainbows. She sees the same beauty in her scars and she does in His rainbows.

According to the American Academy of Dermatology Association, a scar is evidence of how "your body naturally repairs the damage." Further research will show that a cursory search of scars though will generate words such as mend, repair, and heal. In medical terminology, a scar is evidence of healing, not injury. True, an injury has occurred for a scar to appear. However, it is the healing that scars evidence, not the continued wounding.

Those who have been injured, but have no scars are still bleeding or are dead. It is the living, the healed living, that can demonstrate their scars. In speaking of Christ's scars, Charles Spurgeon says this: "Christ wears these scars on His body in heaven as his ornaments. The wounds of Christ are His glories, they are His jewels and his precious things." Further on he claims, "Jesus Christ finds such beauties in His wounds that He will not renounce them, he will wear the court dress in which He wooed our souls, and He will wear the royal purple of His atonement throughout eternity." [16] Davis Mathis at desiringgod.org further argues that "Jesus's scars — as healed wounds — forever tell us of our final victory in Him." [17] So, when Summer says that her scars are evidence that God loves her,

[16] Spurgeon, C. (1859). *The Wounds of Jesus.* New Park Street Pulpit.

[17] Mathis, D. (2019) His Scars Will Never Fade: The Wounds Christ Took to Heaven, Retrieved from https://www.desiringgod.org/articles/his-scars-will-never-fade

she is speaking into a larger, more eternal truth. She is demonstrating an awareness of a profound and essential truth.

Why does it matter? In a world in which the petty annoyances of life make even the most intellectually rigorous doubt the love of God, I see faith that humbles me. No, correct that, Summer's faith in the presence of God shines a light into my own soul that breaks my heart. I look at her faith and I am inspired and encouraged. She is a constant memorial that God loves me. Yes, that God loves me, Mike Hoggatt. How do I know? Because of scars. Yes, there are my own scars that evidence that God has healed me. More importantly, though, are the scars He wears that show He keeps His promises to love, to save, to redeem.

But Martha was pulled away by all she had to do in the kitchen. Later, she stepped in, interrupting them.

"Master, don't you care that my sister has abandoned the kitchen to me? Tell her to lend me a hand."

The Master said, "Martha, dear Martha, you're fussing far too much and getting yourself worked up over nothing. One thing only is essential, and Mary has chosen it—it's the main course, and it won't be taken from her." (Luke 10:40-42 MSG).

I am encouraged by this story from Luke. I imagine Mary sitting at the feet of Jesus transfixed on him as she looks lovingly, longingly even, into his face. Meanwhile, I see Jesus shaking His head as He attempts to get Martha to focus on the essential thing, the main course. I wished that I could relate to Mary more than Martha, but the truth is that I often fuss and get worked up over things that are not the essentials. When I reflect on that, I wonder as well, how many people I have neglected in my fussing over the non-essential.

God brought Summer into our lives when she was just three and a half years-old, and though bringing up a child with her needs might test us, she continues to teach us about the love of God in a way that I have never seen. In truth, I have not always valued all that she brings to my life. Many parents of children with disabilities regularly confront the nefarious "more," that comes from well-wishing friends and family, and random internet trolls (thus I have no social media footprint, but that is a digression I do not have time for). The "more" comes from a focus on what someone could be if only they had more of something, anything. She just needs more (services, therapy, love, education, etc.). It is nefarious, diabolical even. This is not because these things are not good, but rather because there is a thin line between wanting the best for the people we love, and the idea that they are insufficient as they are. Yet, I have fallen prey to this idea as well.

Instead of loving Summer as she was, the proponents of "more" chose to see her as someone in need of fixing. Or, worse yet, they saw her slow speech, maladaptive behaviors, and developmental delays as a fad she was "going through" rather than because of anything related to her unique developmental needs and challenges. We realized then, as now, there was a deep-seated aversion to the possibility that she might be "disabled." Even the word was not something people wanted to verbalize, as if given the word "disabled" voice would make it a reality. And conversely, refusing to acknowledge the word, made everything OK. Therefore, according to this frame of thinking, it was the lack of love or stability (she had been in nine foster placements by the time we brought her home at age 3 ½) that caused her delays, not anything physiological. While that might be true, and in many cases that is true. Our life was more complicated than that.

After a year and a half together, Summer still struggled. She still had challenges. The voice of the dismissers and well-wishers from eighteen months prior crept into our thoughts and turned into accusations about the amount of love we had given or the household we had created. Slowly, the temptation to see her as someone in need of fixing became great. It reared its ugly head at every IEP[18] meeting or contact with developmental services or every session with our behavioral services team.

Maybe we had not loved Summer enough. Maybe a year and a half wasn't enough time. Maybe we were not the right forever family for her. Maybe she was not the right child for us. Doubt, frustration, and anger all show up from time to time amid juggling the various services and supports that accompany a child with disabilities. It becomes very tempting to see your child in terms of what she "isn't" rather than in terms of what she "is." Looking back, I am aghast at the number of times I said in my heart, "if Summer would just . . . (fill in the blank with any age-appropriate behavior)" things would be so much better, or so much easier. I realize now that those times were evidence that I had bought into the lie that my daughter was not sufficient as she was. I know now that these are the lies of the Father of Lies. Lies the plurality of churches adopt. Further, I had made the error of equating easy with good and hard with bad. I had forgotten that although things can be difficult, they can still be good.

First, I had to learn a valuable lesson. Like Martha, in Luke's Gospel, I frequently mistake the immediate for the important. Dur-

---

[18] An IEP is an Individualized Education Plan/Program. This is both a meeting and a document that families and the local school district collaborate on to ensure appropriate special education services.

ing the first eighteen months after Summer came to live with Mandy and I, we experienced a period of change. We were learning behaviors and needs. We were learning our limits and hidden reserves of strengths. We explored interventions, met with therapists, attended IEPs and court dates. In short, we were busy. Not that we weren't enjoying our time together, but we were "fussing" far too much about a great many things. Some of these things we had to do were good and necessary, even required by law. However, the essential things that Jesus talks about operate on a different level. As a result, in our desire to provide all the "little things" we were often missing out on the essential things. Then one day everything changed...

The night before Summer's surgery, around two in the morning, I drove to our house to pick up some clothes for Mandy and me, not knowing how long we would stay in the hospital with her. As I drove down the 55 Freeway through the middle of Orange County, a David Crowder song titled "How He Loves" came on the radio. Throughout the song, the listener is reminded how jealous God is for His people and how beautiful He is. Then in light of my "fussing" and in light of my "more" attitude, which are both evidence of a need for Grace in my life, I heard these lyrics

> *"And we are His portion and He is our prize, Drawn to redemption by the grace in His eyes, If His grace is an ocean, we're all sinking. And heaven meets earth like an unforeseen kiss, And my heart turns violently inside of my chest, I don't have time to maintain these regrets, When I think about the way."*

This was followed by the refrain of *"how He loves us, oh, oh, how He loves us. How He loves us all."*[19]

As I drove home, I was overwhelmed, not with despair, but with Grace. I immediately cried. I was crying so much that I had to get off the freeway as I could not see the road. There I was, in a Del Taco parking lot in Santa Ana at two in the morning, a grown man crying like a baby. At that moment, I did not ask God that Summer have improved speech, behavior, or cognitive faculties. Rather, I thanked God for the gift of Summer's presence in my life, and I prayed for one more opportunity to choose the one essential thing. I prayed for just one more day to sit at her side and enjoy her presence. I was reminded that the presence of those we love, more than their products, is the essential thing. I still had to drive back to the hospital, so feeling a little silly crying in a Del Taco parking lot at two in the morning, I went to the drive thru and order as many Macho items off the Del Taco menu that I could get, and drove back to the hospital.

Often, to create "feelings of belonging" there is a tendency for those of us who live or work alongside people with disabilities, to create and program those opportunities. In short, we fuss about many things: liability, safety, fun activities, volunteers, and more. While there is nothing intrinsically wrong in those things, I wonder if there is a tendency in those times to become Martha and miss the one thing that is needed because we are too busy in the kitchen.

---

[19] MacMillan, J (2005). "How He Loves" [Recorded by David Crowder Band]. On *Church Music* [Audio file]. Retrieved from URL https://genius.com/David-crowder-band-how-he-loves-lyrics

From the Family Archives (July 2009)

Summer has been officially diagnosed with Stage IV Wilms Disease. This is a form of childhood kidney cancer. She has been labeled as Stage IV since the cancer had attached to some lymph nodes surrounding the kidney and the fact that cancer spread into her lungs as well. While the prognosis is serious, it is not without hope. We are fully expecting Summer to make a solid comeback.

However, that comeback will take time. Once Summer recovers from her kidney removal surgery, she will begin a six-month course of treatment that will include chemotherapy and radiation therapy (although the radiation therapy should be completed early on in the treatment program). During her treatment, she will most likely suffer the negative effects of the chemotherapy. This means that she will often be sick as a result of her treatment and will very likely lose her beautiful hair. Another impact of the chemo is the fact that her immune system will be compromised. As a result of this side effect she will be unable to attend school or Sunday school until her treatment course has been completed.

We are grateful for the prayers and support from so many of our friends and family. Summer is amazing. She has a great attitude and never fails to give a hug to each doctor, nurse and hospital staff (and there are dozens) who come to visit on a daily basis. We are very grateful for the gift of her presence. She is a constant reminder that God is a God of "Purpose and Hope." Thank you again for your prayers.

Now, ten healthy years removed from that night, I come home from work differently than before. I still eagerly desire to know what was learned, what progress was made, where struggles and stumbles occurred. Yet now when I come home, I am content with few questions and answers. Rather, Summer will come up to me and ask me "how was work?" I answer her as truthfully as I can and wait for what is next.

She will then ask if I would like a hug from my daughter and if I would like to spend time with her. What father of a teenager doesn't want to hear that? I wish that I can always to say, "yes." Sometimes I must delay that, but when I can, I sit on the couch, Summer comes and sits next to me then leans her head on my shoulder as I wrap my arms around her. We sit in silence for as long as we can. Our mutual gift of presence, our willingness to choose Grace, provides a respite from the false expectations that distract from the essential.

In hindsight, I know that God is teaching me His great counter argument to the world's argument of "more." His great argument is "enough." He is sufficient. He has it all figured out. He is enough. This is why Summer rejoices in her scars. She understands, at a deep level, that God is enough. That God is sufficient. CS Lewis argued that "he who has Christ and many things, has no more than he who has Christ alone."

I have learned through this process the ease at which I, and most people, place our Golden Calves on God's altar is humbling. The frequency that I have allowed my ability (or the ability of others), or wealth, ambition, status, to take Lordship over my life devastates me. Too often I pursue the wrong things. Too often, I allow the gods of this world to be LORD of my life. I need reminders to make the essential thing the main course.

While Summer spent nine months undergoing chemotherapy and radiation treatments, our family was on another journey. Mandy was pregnant the entire time that Summer was undergoing her treatments. In fact Summer's last chemotherapy treatment was completed the same week that her brother was born. During the pregnancy we learned that we were having a boy. We eventually settled on the name Elijah. Elijah translates into My God is the LORD, or My God is Yahweh.

I am inspired by the Biblical account, in I Kings chapter 18, of Elijah as he battles the prophets of Ba'al on Mt. Carmel. The way Elijah stands in defiance against the 450 prophets of Ba'al encourages me. I love, particularly in verse thirty-seven, after Elijah has taunted the false prophets and stood as one man against 450, the manner in which he quietly prays, "Answer me, Lord, answer me, so these people will know that you, Lord, are God, and that you are turning their hearts back again (I King 18:37, NIV)." As God brings fire down from the heavens, the people respond as "they fell prostrate and cried, 'The Lord—he is God! The Lord—he is God!' " (I Kings 18:39, NIV).

We chose the name Elijah as a reminder that "My God is Yahweh" is both a truth and a pursuit. I want the LORD who reigns fire on Mt. Carmel, the LORD who heals cancer, and who heals families to be my God. Is God my pursuit? Does God have lordship over my life? I know I need reminders, but those reminders, those blessings God sends as a sign of His faithfulness amaze me. They also continue to focus me to look at the essentials, the important things in my   life.

The urgent things are not always the essential things: Now What?

Rest is the ultimate humiliation because in order to rest, we must admit we are not necessary, that the world can get along without us, that God's work does not depend on us. -Mike Yaconelli

I first encountered *VeggieTales* in 1994 during the Spring Semester of my Sophomore year at Point Loma Nazarene College. Ever since, I have been a fan, both of the shows as well as their creator, Phil Vischer. I was saddened when, in 2003, Big Ideas (the parent company of *VeggieTales*) filed for bankruptcy. The mergers and legal battles that resulted highlighted the very real, though too often glossed over, truth that Christian businesses are still businesses that can, just like people, easily lose sight of the essential things of Christ.

In 2008, Vischer released a combination memoir and *mea culpa* combined with an instructive approach to focusing on the essentials in business and life titled *Me, Myself, and Bob: A True Story About Dreams, God, and Talking Vegetables*[20]. During the time since its release, I have read and reread the book several times. In its pages I find a man passionate about his savior and eager to follow Him, yet

---

[20] Vischer, P. (2008). *Me, Myself, and Bob: A True Story about Dreams, God, and Talking Vegetables.* Thomas Nelson Inc

who, admittedly, was distracted by the urgent and the seemingly important when he should have been pursuing one thing and one thing only.

Considering Vischer's honest reflections remind me of the danger that happens to our hearts, to our relationships, and to our community when we fail to recognize what is essential in this life. So, what do I do about this? Considering what I have learned in relationship with my daughter, and relying on the words of Vischer, I have identified three important truths to remember while we pursue the essentials.

REMEMBER: GOD IS ENOUGH

There is a lie that we so often believe. The lie that tells us we need more than what God has provided. This lie tempted me, and I almost missed the fact that my daughter, my gift from God, was enough. Vischer, too, fell into this trap. In looking back at his time pursuing his dreams, he writes, "I am very serious when I say this, beware of your dreams, for dreams make dangerous friends. We all have them—longings for a better life, a healthy child, a happy marriage, rewarding work. But dreams are, I have come to believe, misplaced longings. False lovers. Why? Because God is enough." That is it. God is enough. "And" Vischer adds, "He isn't 'enough' because he can make our dreams come true—no, you've got him confused with Santa or Merlin or Oprah. The God who created the universe is enough for us—even without our dreams."

It seems so easy to forget. We scurry around trying to do more. We are so busy trying to improve our station, trying to fix our children, or trying to achieve our version of the American dream that we forget to count our blessings. We forget to trust. We forget that God is enough. Once we accept and lean into the fact that God is enough, the ethereal fantasy of the American dream (be that dream the perfect suburban house, the Ivy-bound perfect child, or the perfect corner office) disappears into vapored mist. Vischer reiterates this point when he says once again, "The God who created the universe is enough for us–even without our dreams...God was enough for the martyrs facing lions and fire–even when the lions and the fire won. And God is enough for you."

REMEMBER: PURSUE OBEDIENCE

If I have tried to please God with my busyness. If I have tried to please God with my acquisition of the American dream, then I might be mistaken and believe that God is judging my accomplishments. I might be mistaken that God favors me more because I can do "more" (whatever that means) for Him. Vischer again nails this point when he writes, "God doesn't love me because of what I can do for him. He just loves me - even when I've done nothing at all." As such, the temptation to "earn" God's love through "fixing" problems that were never problems (i.e. a child with disabilities) fades away in light of God's love.

Yet, even though God calls me to be a faithful servant, as well as the fact that God calls me to be obedient, I too often seek my identity in success, privilege, and power. My identity should be in pursuit of God, in obedience to His word.

In looking back on his own failings in pursuit of something other than obedience, Phil Vischer, succinctly diagnoses the problem. He writes, "Rather than finding my identity in my relationship with God, I was finding it in my drive to do "good work." The more I dove into Scripture, the more I realized that I had been deluded. I had grown up drinking a dangerous cocktail–a mix of the gospel, the Protestant work ethic, and the American dream."

REMEMBER: SLOW DOWN

Once I realize that God is enough, and once I recognize that I must pursue obedience rather than some diabolical fantasy called the American dream, then I have the permission, the release, to simply slow down. Vischer speaks to this epiphany as he writes, "I started to get it. The Christian life wasn't about running like a maniac; it was about walking with God. It wasn't about impact; it was about obedience." This is the point. When Martha frantically scurries about the kitchen, she is missing the point. When Mary sits at the feet of Jesus, she is taking the slow road and "gets it." My daughter tends to take the slow road. Yet, the slow road is often the essential road. As I recognize God's sufficiency, and conform my life to one of obedience, instead of accomplishment, then I can settle into the slow pace of my savior. A gentle pace that is more concerned with relationship and obedience than it is with accomplishment and, so-called success. I also learn that the frenetic pace of accomplishment does not change the world as much as the slow deliberate walk of Jesus.

Lesson #5: Grace and Gratitude are Choices

It was one of those days in which the frustration and struggles associated with parenting a child with disabilities were piling up. Summer was pushing all my buttons. Exasperated, I sat next to her on her bed and decided to be open. Softly, I said, "Summer, I love you, but sometimes it isn't easy being your daddy." (This is nothing new to many of the parents reading this. However, this might come as a bit of a shock to others who simply assume that "God only gives special kids to special parents." This is untrue and dangerous, but I digress.)

Summer smiled at me and said in a question-statement kind of way as if on the one hand she was asking, but on the other, she was restating a principle that we are committed to living by, "but we never stop loving each other because we're a family.?!"

"That's right, sweetheart," I said as she squeezed my neck tightly.

In that moment, we made a choice. The choice was not to have each other in our lives. We had made that choice the day we met eight years earlier when I walked into her group home and saw a three-year-old playing alone at a table. Before introductions could be completed by the social worker, she ran to me and grabbed my neck. It was at that moment that we chose each other. That was a choice, a mutual choice. Yet, relationships are more than a single choice. My marriage to Mandy did not begin and end at the altar when we both chose to say, "I do." Rather, there are daily choices to love, to laugh, to call each other out, to let things go, and to love, honor, and cherish.

Like most relational choices, the choice we made sitting at the edge of her bed that afternoon, however, was one that required an acknowledgment of the gap that existed between us, between any two people in fact. An acknowledgement on her part that she has struggles and areas of weakness, yet simultaneously an acknowledgement that I too have struggles and weaknesses. Despite the acknowledged gap, she reminded me of a commitment to choose Grace. She reminded me that it is not an I/you dynamic, but rather the WE of relationship.

Much of what keeps individuals with disabilities from belonging, whether in personal relationships or more communal ones, is not an issue of difference, but rather an issue of Grace. Often, I hear I-you dynamics in response to disability.

I understand—you are disabled.

I am empathetic—you are in need.

I am a missionary—you are a mission assignment.

This approach places one individual as an actor and one as the recipient of relational dynamics.

However, my experiences have taught me that pity and objectification lurk in this dynamic. I have also learned that Grace lives in the "we" of a relationship. The choice to move from "I" to "we" is a choice of belonging, a choice of friendship, more importantly, it is a choice of Grace.

In fact, choosing Grace allows us to live life together. It is the heartbeat of Friendship if the relationship is to move beyond superficial notions of congeniality into deeper levels of intimacy. Society tends to overlook the struggles of families and individuals affected by disability and/or the trauma of the child welfare system, or, at the very least, minimize and trivialize. This is not friendship; at its best it is what researchers Jennifer Baca and Jeff McNair refer to as "almost friendship."[21] "Almost-friendships" are based on an "I'm-OK-you're-OK" standard. This standard keeps intimacy at bay and results in one member of the relationship feeling superior for their ability to "overlook" the many shortcomings of the other. This is not a friendship. This is pity. Pity quickly turns to resentment and distance.

Grace, however, steps into the gap between us and refuses to back down. Grace says, "Yes, you have shortcomings and struggles; however, we never stop loving each other." It says, "I am here with you in your struggle." It steadfastly proclaims, "I am not leaving your side, no matter how tough it gets."

The surprising thing about Grace, however, is not how difficult it is to give, but how difficult it is to acknowledge one's own need for Grace. Genuine friendships require not only a need to dispense Grace, which some would have you believe is all that is needed to walk alongside those affected by disability. It requires, as well, an acknowledgment of our need for Grace. Learning to receive Grace as dispensed from my daughter with her struggles, strengths, weak-

---

[21] Baca, J. & McNair, J. (2013). Almost friends. *Journal of the Christian Institute on Disability*, 2(1), 27-41.

nesses, dreams, and passions is something God has been teaching me since the day we met. This is one of many blessings that life together with those affected by disabilities brings, as we mutually step toward one another in Grace.

Often choosing Grace means simply choosing to be present and accept the presence of those around us. Presence is something that each of us can offer on a fairly equitable scale, regardless of perceived strengths or weaknesses. Too often, in our fussing over the many things, we deny ourselves the gift of presence. Much like Martha, the Church has been fussing in the kitchen and missing out on the essential presence of Christ in the room. For me, it took the possibility of losing that presence to cancer to understand fully the essential nature and importance of presence as a gift of Grace.

Life together is choosing presence over busy-ness. Grace recognizes that relationship is made in mutual presence, not mutual accomplishments. I love being married. Mandy and I have been married for over eighteen years. During this time, we have found many things on which we see eye-to-eye. We have found many activities in which we both whole-heartedly enjoy. Yet, there are differences. We do not marry or partner with mirror images of ourselves. Yet, we are called to live in relationship. Relationships are the ongoing analogy in which God explains Himself to us. It is through the prism of parenthood and marriage in which we learn about God. I rely, once again, on N.T. to express the role relationship plays in our understanding of God's creation and our role within it. Wright says, "[r]elationship was part of the way in which we were meant to be fully human, not for our own sake, but as part of a much larger scheme of things."

It is easy to get frustrated when I focus on myself and all I bring to a relationship. If we're honest, we have all had that moment when we think we're putting in more than we're taking out. This thinking leads to isolation and bitterness. We think this way at work when we feel that we are doing more than "our share." We feel this way in our family dynamics when our spouse, kids, parents, friends will not meet us "half-way."

I am reminded of those three stories about lost things. These stories remind me that the Grace and Love of God are pursuits designed to close the gap between God and the thing that was lost (e.g. me). Grace in relationships is pursuit. It is a model of God's pursuit of us. The book of Hosea is a story picture of this pursuit. Regardless of what we may assume. We are not Hosea in this story, we (each of us) are decidedly in the Gomer role. It is only God's pursuit of us that allows us into a relationship with Him. If this is the model of relationship God displays, it seems obvious, though by no means easy, what I should model in my own relationships.

Look at the spokes on a tire. When do they move closer to one another? They do not move closer while out on the rim. Rather, as they move toward the center, they necessarily move closer one to another. Our lives are laid out in much the same way. As we move toward the center. In other words, as we pursue God, we cannot help but move closer to one another. I move closer to my wife as I pursue God. My intimacy with her is a direct consequence of my pursuit of God. Likewise, as she pursues God, she can be in a deeper relationship with me. This is not because suddenly she likes me more. Rather, she can more freely and liberally cover my shortcomings (of which there are many) with Grace and Love. This is something difficult to accomplish when we are out on the rim. When I pursue God, I am reminded of Paul's admonishment to husbands is to "love your wives, just as Christ also loved the church and gave Himself up for her" (Ephesians 5:25, NASB). This call to love is only possible when I pursue Christ first.

This pursuit of God is central to any relationship. In fact, as I pursue God and become an imitator of Christ, I can enter relationships I had never dreamed of and to be better at relationships. In the first book of Corinthians chapter thirteen, Paul presents the famous passage on love. Picking up the text in verse two of the New International Version, Paul writes,

> *"If I have the gift of prophecy and can fathom all mysteries and all knowledge, and if I have a faith that can move mountains, but do not have love, I am nothing. If I give all I possess to the poor and give over my body to hardship that I may boast, but do not have love, I gain nothing.*
>
> *Love is patient, love is kind. It does not envy; it does not boast; it is not proud. It does not dishonor others; it is not self-seeking; it is not easily angered; it keeps no record of wrongs. Love does not delight in evil but rejoices with the truth. It always protects, always trusts, always hopes, always perseveres."*

These words are famous. They are embroidered on pillows and spoken at weddings. Yet, I wonder how often these words are internalized. If I am to be an imitator of God (Ephesians 5:1) and if God is love (1 John 4:7-8), then I should embody love in my relationships. Yes, even with those who are a bit tough to love. Try something for me, just a quick experiment. Please...First, in the following section from 1 Corinthians 13, fill in the blanks with your name. Second, think about a difficult relationship you have and include that person in this passage.

> *Mike is patient with Summer, Mike is kind to Summer. Mike does not envy Summer's attention, Mike does not boast about his own accomplishments, Mike is not proud. Mike does not dishonor Summer, Mike is not self-seeking, Mike is not easily angered by Summer, Mike keeps no record of Summer's wrongs. Mike does not delight in evil but rejoices with the truth. Mike always protects, always trusts, always hopes, always perseveres."*

When I do this exercise several things immediately strike me and leave me gobsmacked. First, I do not love as well as I think I do. Second, I am more thankful for God's amazing grace. In fact, considering my woeful performance regarding love, I am more deeply amazed by God's grace and love.

Something else happens as I move toward the center. Another amazing thing happens. As I pursue the middle, I stop focusing on the other spokes and how different they are from me or how "less than perfect" they might appear. As I pursue the center, as I pursue God, I am overwhelmed with thankfulness for the opportunity to be on this journey. I also notice that the people near the center look nothing like I assumed they would. I realize that they seldom look like me.

As I fix my eyes on God, I learn more about who God is. In fact, it is much easier to recognize God's image represented in my neighbor as I pursue God. I recognize that I am not the end-all-be-all of God's image. The closer I get to God, the more I realize that there

119

is a diversity of people created in God's image. The more I note the vast sea of images before me, people bearing the imago Dei, the more I learn of the rich and vast nature of my creator. As I near the center, I note that those around the Savior do not all look like me or even look the way I expected them to look. In fact, where Christ sits, those society have disregarded find a place to be. The one society has oppressed finds safety. As I approach Christ, I realize that I had the whole notion of "marginalization" wrong.

This I find interesting because Jesus told me where He would be. "Then the King will say, 'I'm telling the solemn truth: Whenever you did one of these things to someone overlooked or ignored, that was me—you did it to me'." (Matthew 25:37-40, MSG)

When I made myself the hub, I wrongly assumed that the people I thought too different, too radically different, to be part of my life were out on the margins. Yet, as I pursue Christ and His Kingdom first, I realize that I was the one on the margins and those people I had disregarded, where actually at the center, because they were with Jesus. Jesus is the center of all things. If I am with Jesus, I can then not be on the margins, unless I am speaking of the Kingdom of Man, not the Kingdom of Heaven, for when the Kingdom of Heaven is near, the margins (and marginalized) look different.

This has made me think about Summer. Summer embraces those who look different. She wants a relationship with those who others may neglect. It is a divine Grace that flows, allowing her to connect to the imago Dei in another. I then realize that if I choose Grace, then the people I surround myself should reflect that. How can I know the image of God if I only surround myself with one type of person? If there is no diversity in my life of race, creed, ability, ethnicity, and color then am I not limiting my understanding of God through the presence of His creation?

Both the terms "Grace" and "Gratitude" share similar etymologies. Both derive from the Latin word *"gratia."* Whereas *Grace* translates as favor, esteem, or regard; *Gratitude* branches off of the root and most typically translates as thankfulness or goodwill. In essence, I show (or should) gratitude (thankfulness or goodwill) for the grace (favor or regard) in my life. Both grace and gratitude are not mere responses to some external stimuli, they are choices or decisions. They are acts of the will. God grants me the grace to know him, to love him, and to be in fellowship with him through the sacrifice of His son. I respond with either indifference or gratitude. Either is a choice. Both are an attitude of the heart rather than a reflex. Gratitude is not saying "thank you." Rather, it is being thankful. Saying "thank you" is akin to say "bless you" when someone sneezes. In our lives, the ability to extend grace and the ability to show gratitude is a response, not to what we have been given (either biologically or materially), but simply to who God is and whether our hearts are oriented toward Him or toward ourselves, and our self-interest.

Being the father of a child with an intellectual disability, a child with autism, a child who has suffered abuse in a cruel and indifferent child welfare system, and a child who has struggled through life against the evil that is cancer, it is a challenge. It is even more of a challenge when I hear "there but for the grace of God go I" comments in response to any of the above. My heart breaks when I know that people are expressing gratitude toward God that they are not my daughter, or that their child has not lived my daughter's life, or that they do not have her diagnoses and/or experiences. Yet, Summer teaches me continually what genuine gratitude is considering God's grace.

Each year, the kids make a Thanksgiving garland made with strips of paper connected one to another. Each strip identifies something that they are thankful for. Each year Mandy collects these lists of thanksgiving and hangs it from our fireplace mantel for the Thanksgiving season. Last year, this was Summer's list. I share this list, not merely as an example, but to highlight the deeper gratitude in which Summer lives, and to which I aspire.

I am thankful that I survived kidney cancer

Summer is thankful for life. That is it. Life is a gift from God. The other aspects (skills, abilities, accolades, etc.) are mere window dressing on the simple gift that is life. To denigrate life to some Shakespearean amalgamation of reason and skills is to miss sight of "the gift." Summer does not possess the skills and abilities many of her typically developing peers do. Yet, she is ever grateful (again the same root of *gratia*) for life. Life as a gift from her Heavenly Father. While I try to accumulate or progress, Summer is content, and grateful, to experience life as a gift of God. Oh, that I would do the same.

I am thankful for Rainbows.

When Summer expresses gratitude for rainbows, she is not merely expressing thankfulness for something that is aesthetically pleasing, though she is indeed doing so. When Summer was young, she would point out any rainbow she saw with excitement. "Look, Daddy," she would squeal, "a rainbow."

"Yes," I would respond and follow up with a question, "What do rainbows mean?"

"God always keeps His promises," she would answer with the widest of grins.

So, when she says that she is thankful for rainbows, she is saying both that she is grateful for the beauty of God's created world, but also for His willingness to keep His word.

Her gratitude for God's promises considering her life experiences is something I strive to emulate in light of His grace.

I am thankful for family.

As I explained in chapter two, Summer understands where she belongs. Her statement of gratitude for family connections to both her thankfulness for life and for God's willingness to keep His promises. Summer knows what it is like not to have a family, so her gratitude for a family is so much more sincere. When I am annoyed by those in my family, Summer pulls me back to a point in which I strive to, like Mary, meditate on the essential things.

I am thankful for making my first pizza from pizza dough

Just a few days prior to Thanksgiving, our good friends Greg and Amanda came over to make dinner with us. Amanda brought over the ingredients to make personal pizzas. The kids were delighted for the opportunity. Summer was grateful, not for the pizza, though it was tasty. Rather, she was thankful for being allowed to contribute, to create. As an image-bearer of God, I am, unlike other creations, the ability to create. Summer recognized this and was thankful for it. She was not thankful that she made the best pizza ever. Rather, she was thankful that she created. Too often individuals with disabilities have everything done for them and are, therefore, not offered the opportunity to create for themselves. Summer reminds me that the ability to create is both essential to her status as an image-bearer of

God and essential to the dignity she deserves to be afforded in this world.

I am thankful for sleeping in on vacation and weekends

I think too often I complicate the pleasures in life. Summer reminds me that simple pleasures are often the most enjoyable. Instead of being overly "refined" or "cultured" or "sophisticated," Summer reminds me to let go and enjoy the simple pleasures that life affords.

I am thankful for no thunderstorms tonight

Once as we were traveling along a lengthy road trip, Summer let us know that, in her own words, "there are only two things that scare me... Black holes and thunderstorms." First, I find that encouraging considering her life. She has experienced so many things that would scare the bravest of people. Yet, she both recognizes the difference between those things that make us nervous and those things from which we should be fearful. Her thankfulness for the lack of thunderstorms is a recognition that God has His hand on her. That God protects her and has the world under control. Too often, I try to "control" things. Yet, Summer reminds me to lean into the reality that God has the world, even the Thunderstorms under His control.

I am thankful for the stars (you can see them to find out the shape)

I am thankful for monarch butterflies (they are very pretty)

Both items show the pure wonder that Summer possesses. I long to regain the sense of wonder that I had for God and His creation when I was a child. Too often I fail to appreciate her sense of wonder. I am often too impatient when she stops to make me look up at the stars, or when she stops us on a walk to check out a butterfly along a path. Yet, each time she shows her gratitude and wonder for an act of God's creation, I am humbled. I realize that my agenda, my list of things-to-do, and my priorities are better-realigned when I stop to show proper gratitude for all that God has deigned to share with the world.

I am thankful for making people's day (which is making them feel welcomed)

Summer can make people feel loved. To make people feel they are important, that they are cared for and that they are important in the scheme of creation. She knows that she does this and any. She knows too, that this ability to share and comfort others is a gift from God. In a world that patronizes people with disabilities, that marginalizes their gifts, that trivializes their contributions, Summer recognizes that she was created for a purpose by her creator to do great things. Her gratitude to her creator reminds me to seek God's will in order that I too might live my purpose.

Summer's gratitude is a pure exchange between her and her God. She does not qualify her gratitude compared to others, which I too often do. Rather she sees her life, and gratitude, as a choice and decision of the heart in an understanding of her status as a creation of God, as an image-bearer of God, and, most importantly, as a child of God. I am learning, though, often with great difficulty, to do likewise.

From the Family Archives (Thanksgiving 2008)

Sometimes it is difficult to understand how God works. We can easily question how God can use a particular situation, mistake or choose to His glory. This is part of the human condition. We so easily put God in a box and we don't even realize it. We look at our choice or our situation and assume since we can't see any good in it, God can't either. Yet, God repeatedly shows us mercy through our struggles and weakness. This has been true in my personal journey, but also in our family's journey.

Several years ago, my wife and I took our four-year-old niece to Disneyland. Near the end of the day, we stood on Main Street to watch the parade. It had been a long day, and she didn't accept my offer to sit on my shoulders. She wanted to be independent and stand on her own. As we stood there a little while, I noticed her getting frustrated. Upon closer look, I realized that while she could hear the band play and the crowd cheer, all she could see was people's knees and butts. From her perspective, there wasn't much of a parade. In fact, hearing a lot of loud noises when all you can see are knees and butts pretty much stinks (no pun intended). I knew I had to help her out and change her perspective. Without waiting for her approval, I reached down, grabbed her by the waist and hoisted her on top of my shoulders. Now she had the best seat in the crowd. She could see everything. Now when she waved, Cinderella waved back. She was laughing and clapping. While nothing around her changed, her perspective had changed, and that made all the difference. For her, it was as if the entire parade had been made for her, now that she could see it more clearly. And quickly her tears turned to thankfulness.

Occasionally in our lives, all we can see are knees and butts. We need some change of perspective. Whether it has been choices, I have made or situations in my life; it has blessed me that God has taken the time to lift me out of the crowd so I can see the parade. God has let me know that while I can't see it, there are good things happening around me. As independent as I want to be, sometimes I need the help of His perspective. Sometimes I need to sit on His shoulders in order to enjoy the parade He has orchestrated. And for those shoulders, I am thankful.

Waiting for our child has been difficult. We have been frustrated and disappointed. All we have seen are knees and butts. However, that is just our perspective. When we sit on God's shoulders we see that this waiting has given us an opportunity to encourage others down this road. We see that opportunities to connect with faith-based organizations in the advocacy of all foster and adoptive children, particularly those labeled with special needs, has been part of God's divine plan. We also know that God has used this time to mold our hearts and prepare us for our forever family. And for that plan, I am thankful.

My journey to this point has been filled with people, places, situations and challenges that all served in one way or another to inform my head and my heart. Looking back at the choices and struggles I dealt with individually as well as those Mandy and I dealt with together, I now understand what St. Paul is trying to convey when he speaks of God's strength being made perfect in our weakness. I know that my weaknesses and challenges could never have led me to this point without God's intervention. I know that when all we could see were knees and butts, God has granted us the opportunity to see the parade. And for that perspective, I am thankful.

Regardless of how my journey has led me here, there is something I know beyond question. As I look at my daughter's face, I know that I am where I was meant to be. I know that all the hoops, struggles, challenges, waiting, disappointments, knees and butts (e.g. social service agencies) led me to the exact point I am today. God used them all as markers and signposts on my journey so I would be right where I am. I know this is the perfect place. In hindsight, had my path been different, had my journey been easier, I might not be where I am sitting beside my wife and my child. That would be a tragedy. There is no place I would rather be. And for that I am thankful.

Grace and Gratitude are Choices: Now What?

Gratitude for the seemingly insignificant—a seed—this plants the giant miracle.— Ann Voskamp

I continue to marvel at how much my daughter teaches me daily of Grace, God's Great Grace. Likewise, I marvel at how her life continues to teach me to be grateful and to express gratitude in my life. As I learn more about God's Amazing Grace, I am made more aware of what I must be grateful for.

Point Loma Nazarene College, where I attended, required that students attend chapel three times a week. Different speakers would come, some from within the college and some from without. Every year, though, the most popular speaker, the one that many of us looked forward to, was a former Franciscan priest and recovering alcoholic named Brennan Manning. Manning's writings would have a significant impact on my understanding of grace. While I have enjoyed much of his writing, I think *The ragamuffin gospel: Good news for the bedraggled, beat-up, and burned out is my favorite*[22]. Maybe it's the substance of the book or perhaps it's because I have also been

---

[22] Manning, B. (1990). *The ragamuffin gospel: Good news for the bedraggled, beat-up, and burnt out*. Multnomah Books.

encouraged and inspired by Rich Mullins and his Ragamuffin Band. Regardless, I see a message of grace I cannot ignore, but one for which I am grateful.

CHOOSE GRACE

As I learn about God's Grace, I am more able to choose that Grace and to accept who I am in light of God's grace. Manning explains it this way, "Genuine self-acceptance is not derived from the power of positive thinking, mind games, or pop psychology. It is an act of faith in the grace of God." Choosing God's Grace for my life allows me to move forward into what He has in store. In fact, Manning further argues, "When we wallow in guilt, remorse, and shame over real or imagined sins of the past, we are disdaining God's gift of grace."

Rather, we must live in deep grace which acknowledges that we are mere "ragamuffins" (or to use Mike Yaconelli's word "riff-raff) before a king. Yet, it also requires that I learn to acknowledge that "my deepest awareness of myself is that I am deeply loved by Jesus Christ and I have done nothing to earn or deserve it." Choosing to live in this grace precedes my ability to extend this grace to others. I must live in this grace to fully appreciate or show gratitude for it.

SHOW GRACE

As Summer has reminded me of God's amazing grace, and my need for it, I have grown in my understanding of my need to extend that grace to others. I wish that I could say that I am awesome at it. Unfortunately, I regularly find that I have too much in common with the "unmerciful servant" Jesus described in Matthew 18:21-35. I have been forgiven so much. I have been given so much grace, yet I am so quick to make unreasonable demands of those around me.

I must show grace. I must extend grace. Even if my local church refuses to offer grace to my daughter and invite her in, I must show grace. Even if, even if, even if. . .Yes, even when someone does not deserve it, otherwise it wouldn't be grace. "Grace," Manning reminds us, "is the active expression of His love." Moreover, he argues, "something is radically wrong when the local church rejects someone accepted by Jesus."

I show Grace, not by ignoring differences, gaps, and shortcomings. If the difference does not exist, neither does the need for grace. Rather, I show grace when I recognize the gap between us and move to close that gap with love.

CHOOSE GRATITUDE

As I seek to embrace the grace that God extends toward me, and as I choose to recognize how great my need for grace continues to be, I am overwhelmed by gratitude for my savior. Again, this realization that I am a ragamuffin (e.g. riff-raff) provokes a deeper sense of gratitude. Manning explains: 'The deeper we grow in the Spirit of Jesus Christ, the poorer we become–the more we realize that everything in life is a gift." Yes, everything in life is a gift. It took me too long to realize the gift that was my daughter's life. Even longer to realize that her so-called disability has been a blessing that none of us in our family would exchange. It took a long time to come to this realization that Summer in her entirety is a gift of God's love.

I had arrogantly decided that God's love must look a particular way. I had created a world in which God's love was taken for granted. I failed to be grateful for the wonder. Manning reminds us that "When God's love is taken for granted, we paint Him into a corner and rob Him of the opportunity to love us in a NEW AND SURPRISING way, and faith begins to shrivel and shrink." This was our danger. Yet, as we choose to be grateful for all of God's new, surprising, and beautiful gifts, I see the world and its Creator in NEW and SURPRISING ways.

SHOW GRATITUDE

I am grateful for the amazing grace of God. I am grateful for a God who loves me even when I don't always "get it." I am grateful for a God who loves riff-raff and ragamuffins like me. Yet, being grateful and showing gratitude is not the same. I show gratitude by giving voice to grace. I do not simply say thank you. Rather, I live with gratitude. I begin to look to see and be grateful for the grace notes in my life. I do not mean that I am naïve and pretend that pain does not exist. No, I recognize the pain, I journey through the pain, yet I also seek to find traces of heaven. My ever-optimistic daughter has taught me to look at the world and speak gratitude into the lives of others not by flattering or deceit, but with an honest recognition of the gifts that ALL bring to the table. I show gratitude when I seek the gifts that another is uniquely equipped to provide, regardless of the false valuation the world prescribes.

Most importantly though, I show gratitude to my savior when I show compassion. I show compassion because I have been shown such compassion. I have been lost and my savior searched me out. Like the prodigal's father who threw a party, or the finder of lost coins who rejoiced, my savior models gratitude even when I have been ungrateful. He shows compassion even when I have caused pain. Compassion is the ultimate demonstration of one who is grateful for the love of a Savior. Manning writes, "Compassion for others is not a simple virtue because it avoids snap judgements of right or wrong, good or bad, hero or villain: It seeks truth in all its complexity. Genuine compassion means that in empathizing with the failed plans and uncertain loves of the other person, we send out the vibration, 'Yes, ragamuffin, I understand. I've been there too'."

Lesson #6: Fear Not

Ask anyone who has endured the treatments associated with Cancer and they will let you know of the pain these treatments can cause. They will let you know of the grind of following a strict protocol. Each treatment impacts an individual in particular ways. In ways only they understand. In addition to the struggle associated with the prescribed regimen is the toll this treatment takes on the psyche. There are questions, "Is all this pain going to be worth it?" This question speaks to the struggle to see beyond the treatment. It speaks to the months of life lost to treatment. It speaks to the sinister equation [how many additional days of life this treatment may provide-how many days are lost in treatment = is it worth it?]. Other questions arise, such as "Will I have to do this again if cancer comes back?" There are also immediate questions, "If I have chemo on Thursday, will I be well enough to see my wife or husband or brother or friend or sister at their birthday party on Sunday?" Cancer, as a disease, is all-consuming. It is pervasive, so these questions are a natural outgrowth of the process. The questions speak to the fear that is Cancer's bedfellow.

When Mandy, Summer, and I began our journey into the world of chemotherapy and radiation, we were afraid. All of us. Yes, we trusted God. But we were afraid. We didn't know if our family would survive. We had only been a family for about a year and a half and felt like we were just getting to know each other. Could this be over? Could our daughter, for whom life had been so unpredictable, moving from place to place, encounter one more surprising obstacle too much to overcome? The reality of our fears did not remove our faith. Yet, the fear of the unknown became part of our discourse as we navigated treatment, family, and life, even as trust in a merciful God remained.

During Summer's initial surgery, she had a port placed in her chest. The port would be used to administer the chemotherapy once Summer recovered from surgery. Once Summer was released from the hospital our routine became blood work on Wednesday and out-patient infusion (chemotherapy) on Fridays. We would ultimately do this routine for nine months. Each of these visits required Summer to have her port "accessed.' Basically, this meant that a specially designed needle would break the skin right above her port and, more or less, slide into place. There are a lot of advantages to having blood work and chemo done through a port. Yet for a little girl, one disadvantage was having to watch this menacing looking device coming straight for you.

Summer was terrified each time she had to be accessed. She would squirm and cry, "no, no, no."

To keep her still, I would crawl up onto the hospital bed and wrap my arms and legs around her like a spider. I would hold her tight and whisper in her ear. I would say, "I know it's scary, but it's almost over." I would say, "I know this is scary, but you're so brave."

As soon as they accessed her and the tape applied to keep everything in place, she would look at me, still tears in her eyes, and say, "Nunner brave?" I would squeeze her tight, and smile, still tears in my eyes, and say, "Yes, yes you are."

Mind you, with lab work and chemo, we went through this routine twice a week for nine months. About 60-75 times. Each time we finished, after I let her go, she would approach the nurse or lab technician that had just been the focus of terror only minutes before and give them a hug. Along with the hug, she would say, "it's ok, nunner brave."

Who is nunners, you might ask? Well, when Summer arrived in our family, as I mentioned before, she had very few words. In fact, not only did she have very few words, she had significant oral motor issues. This means she had trouble with both speech and language development. She had particular trouble pronouncing the letter S at the beginning of words, among a few other challenges. So, for the first few years of her life, she called herself "nunners," in her attempt to say the word, "Summer."

Summer referencing herself as "nunners" stems from the myriad of cognitive and developmental issues she faced at the time and continues to face ten years later. Why should that matter? It matters because, during the early stages of our diagnosis and treatment for Cancer, we regularly heard "Well, it's probably a good thing she doesn't understand what's going on." This statement (or something similar) was repeated time and time again by people we loved and who loved us. Yet, while it came from a good place, a well-intentioned place, it betrayed a worldview about what life is like for disabled individuals.

The statement argues that Summer is too impaired, disabled, etc (fill in your word of preference) to be afraid. The central issue is that the statement is more about comforting the individual who made the statement than it is about comforting either Summer or her parents. A further problem is fundamental to who Summer is. "Nunner brave" is only true in light of fear.

A brick wall is not brave for withstanding the wrecking ball. Only a recognition of what the wrecking ball can or will do allows for fear and subsequent bravery in the face of that fear. By minimizing Summer's fear, or at least her ability to be afraid, she is being robbed of her bravery and her courage.

"Nunners brave" was not a statement made in ignorance. Rather, it was made in light of fear. Did she understand all the implications associated with her diagnosis or her treatment? Of course not. Do you understand the implications of whatever situation you are encountering? Probably not. Yet, you can also be brave. Summer knew fear. She understood that the medicine made her sick. She understood that a sharp needle coming at her chest was scary. She understood that grownups hovering over her were intimidating. Yet she chose, yes chose, to face the fear. She chose courage in the face of fear. She chose bravery, not because she knew no fear, but because she understood that there was something to be afraid of.

Summer has seen evil. Yes, Cancer is evil, but so is abuse both at the hands of caregivers and the child welfare system. She has seen terrors. She understands, to the best of her ability, how close cancer came to ending her life. Yet, she knows that "God was there." She knows that God was bigger than her terror.

That is the point. If she has nothing to be afraid of than God is small. If she has nothing to fear, she has no need for courage. What Summer continues to show, not only in her views, but in the way, others engage with her, is that the obstacles, struggles, perceived deficits, and all other negative attributes are part of who she is. To negate her fear negates her bravery. To negate her struggles likewise negates her resilience, her strength, and her courage.

Please note that I do not argue that Summer's disability allows her to be brave or an overcomer. Summer does not overcome her disability. Her disability is an amalgamation of perceptions and obstacles put in her path by a society that intersects with certain functional limitations. It is not Summer who needs to overcome disability. Rather, Summer persists despite society's imposition of obstacles (e.g. disability). This is important as I will explain later.

Summer has fear, but she is brave despite the fear. She persists. She never gives up. She recognizes that things can be hard and that doing hard things allows for more pride in the effort. I enjoy being Summer's father. I love being able to spend time with my daughter. One Sunday afternoon, Mandy came into the living room and saw Summer and I sitting arm-in-arm on the sofa. She asked, "What are you guys up to?"

Summer responded, "Just hanging out watching football with my dad." I beamed with pride. I love those moments. Yet, despite those moments, I recognize that living with a child who has experienced what she has experienced and the developmental challenges she struggles to master, is difficult. I would not want our life any other way, but that is not to say that life can't be difficult.

This leads to a problem. It pains me to hear cliched responses to Summer's struggle because of her being "differently-abled" or "handicapable." It further pains me when someone tells me in response to a voiced frustration of mine or a struggle that I might share that "all kids are [blank]," (fill in the blank with your favorite challenging behavior), they are attempting to minimize my hurt, my suffering, my pain, and my journey. They are not really trying to comfort me as much as excuse themselves from entering my story and being present. Typically, I smile and nod, too weak to fight. However, I want to answer with "yes, but your child may go to church with the youth group," or "you don't have to navigate special education or social security or Medicaid alongside your child." Disability scholar and advocate Anjali J Forber-Pratt argues "*these euphemisms are doing more harm than good because they reinforce the negative stereotype that disability should be feared. This intentional avoidance of the term disability sends the message that there's something inherently negative or bad about having a disability.*"[23]

This avoidance leads to problems. It minimizes my reality. It scolds Summer, or by extension her parents, for acknowledging that life can be hard when someone does not fit social ideals. It reduces the ability of the "minimizer" to participate in Christian compassion.

Compassion comes from a root that means "to suffer alongside of." Christians have been commanded to be compassionate as God is compassionate (Luke 6:36). Now follow me here. If I neglect the suffering of my fellow person, I distance myself from my ability to be compassionate. I can pity another, but to truly be compassionate, I must acknowledge the suffering of another and walk alongside that person. Compassion does not always require the removal of suffering, though that is aspirational. It does, however, require recognition and willingness to bear that pain in fellowship. Therefore, if I minimize your pain, I keep myself from compassion and therefore, I

---

[23] Forber-Pratt, A. J (2019). *Yes, you can call me disabled. Quartz.* Retrieved from https://qz.com/1632728/yes-you-can-call-me-disabled/

place myself in disobedience to the command to be compassionate as stated in Luke 6:36.

Summer is teaching me to not only be brave, something she does all the time. She is teaching me that all my story--every part, good, bad, and indifferent—is precious. This doesn't mean I relish the pain and suffering or over-dramatize them. It does not mean that I provide a cliched response to the trials and pains of life. It means, however, that these parts that others would relegate to the trash heap of my life are redeemed by God and able to be used according to His purposes.

When Mandy and I married, we explicitly stated that we would love, honor, and cherish one another for *Better* or *Worse*. We acknowledge, as countless others have before and since, that a relationship exists within the good and bad. We made a commitment to be wholly part of each other's story. We not only promised that we would celebrate triumphs together, but that we would also comfort one another when bad things would come our way. We also promised that it wasn't possible to be in a relationship only part way, or for only the good parts. A complete relationship does not pick and choose. If it does, it is not a relationship of quality of standing.

Likewise, when individuals are reduced to caricatures of "nice" things, they are not seen as individuals at all. When Summer, or any person with a disability or parent/caregiver of someone with a disability, has their fears, struggles, pains, or obstacles minimized or ignored they themselves are also minimized or ignored.

Summer will tell anyone who listens that her story is a miracle. It is a miracle, not because it was easy or because it was a sweet experience. She will tell you that God heals. She will tell you she was healed because "God was there." That's it. Faced with insurmountable pain and struggle, she knows that God was, and is bigger than her fear. This allows her to be brave. It is a damnable shame when others try to rob her of that truth, regardless of the intention.

Summer describes herself as having "autimism." She also identified as having a disability. When I introduced her to a colleague or talk about friends who work alongside individuals with disabilities, Summer will ask, "do they know that I have a disability?" Regardless of the situation, Summer is not ashamed of labels. Autism or Intellectual Disability are not labels to be discarded or embarrassed of. Rather, she owns her identity. She is proud of who she is. She feels no stigma assigned to her diagnosis. She knows that the significant problems associated with disability are those imposed by others.

Summer has been called "differently-abled," and "special needs." Yet, both fail to capture who she is and how she identifies. Both are attempts to minimize her needs due to the speaker's discomfort with the word "disability" rather than hers.

The disability rights community has noted that in both social media and in more academic writings. In a 2016 NPR interview, disability rights activist Lawrence Carter-Long was asked what people miss when they minimize obstacles and/or disabilities. He argues that *"If you 'see the person not the disability' you're only getting half the picture."* He argues that "...*to suggest disability is simply a 'difference' and has no impact on a person's life is a very privileged position to take. Most disabled people don't have that luxury."[24]*

As a result, Carter-Long has developed the **DISABLED. #say the word** campaign to promote a dialogue about the need to use the word, own the word, and refuse to stigmatize the word.

As a parent of a disabled child, I do not get to euphemize our familial struggle away by use of cliche. Rather, if I am to wholly love my daughter, I must embrace all of who she is. I must embrace her strengths and weaknesses (as she does mine). I must acknowledge that she is disabled. I must acknowledge that she learns differently, and that she has struggles that I do not experience. If I do not, I cannot partner with her to navigate a complex world. If I do not, I cannot instill in her the sense that she was created by God for a purpose. She is not defective, nor is she broken because she carries a diagnosis.

"Well, I don't see Summer as disabled," well-intentioned individuals might argue. Yet, as Psychologist Erin Andrew and associates, argue in a recent article in the *Journal Rehabilitation Psychology*: *"These efforts to avoid using the word disability paradoxically reveal actual prejudices and biases against people with disabilities."* They continue, noting that, *"The implication is that disability is negative, and the individual defies the undesirable stereotypes held by the observer."[25]*

So, while I understand the tendency to avoid disabled realities, it is not helpful. Again, it places her story on the margins. It

---

[24] Carter-Long, L. as cited in King, B. (2016) Disabled.Just #saytheword. Retrieved from https://www.npr.org/sections/13.7/2016/02/25/468073722/disabled-just-saytheword
[25] Andrews, E. E., Forber-Pratt, A. J., Mona, L. R., Lund, E. M., Pilarski, C. R., & Balter, R. (2019). #SaytheWord: A disability culture commentary on the erasure of "disability". *Rehabilitation psychology.*

places her on the sidelines. She becomes something cute and ancillary to the "real" things in life. Yet, I argue that Summer's insistence on her own bravery is a courageous response in the face of fear. Those who attempt to minimize or marginalize her story are doing so out of their own fears and could learn so much more Summer than she from them.

Nunner Brave. Again, Summer was brave, not because she did not see the danger. She was brave because she faced her dangers with courage. In the sixth chapter of the second book of Kings, we read a story of bravery in the face of threat. The king of the Arameans has been making war against Israel. Every time the king of the Arameans would devise a plan, it was as if the Israelites were in his council. He could not figure out why his plans were always compromised. He challenged his officers, who claimed innocence. They informed the king that Elisha, the prophet of God, was telling the king of Israel, "the very words you speak in your bedroom" (2 Kings 6:12). So, the king of the Arameans decided to take out Elisha by sending his army to Dothan, where Elisha lived.

> "Then [the king of the Arameans] sent horses and chariots and a strong force there. They went by night and surrounded the city. When the servant of the man of God got up and went out early the next morning, an army with horses and chariots had surrounded the city. "Oh no, my lord! What shall we do?" the servant asked." (2 Kings 6:14-15, NIV).

Imagine this. You wake up and go outside to do your morning chores. When your eyes adjust to the sun, you see the armies of the enemy encamped around you. The chariots and horses of the Arameans had surrounded the town of Dothan. The servant runs into the house, frantically calling out to his master. The servant is afraid. The servant recognizes the threat the armies of the Arameans pose.

So, what does Elisha do? Does he minimize the threat? No, in fact, the threat remains. Elisha does not minimize the servant's fears. Rather, he responds in verse sixteen, "Don't be afraid." In other words, he asks the servant to be brave, because as Elisha concludes, "[t]hose who are with us are more than those who are with them."

I cannot overstate the importance of the next verse. Elisha does not pray that the Arameans will disappear. He simply prays that this servant recognizes, in his fear, who God is and what power God possesses. Verse seventeen picks up the story, *"And Elisha prayed, "Open his eyes, Lord, so that he may see." Then the Lord opened the servant's eyes, and he looked and saw the hills full of horses and chariots of fire all around Elisha."*

In essence, Elisha tells his servant the very thing that Summer learned in a hospital room several thousand years later. Yes, the danger is real. Yes, the threat is real. Yes, it is scary, but God is here. So, fear not.

Fear not. It is the central message of Christmas. The angel comes to Zacharias, to Mary, to Joseph, and to the Shepherds with the same message. . .FEAR NOT.

The angel tells Zacharias, "Fear not, thy prayers have been heard." (Luke 1:13, NIV)

Mary is told to, "Fear not, you have found favor with God." (Luke 1:30, NIV)

145

Joseph is told that God's hand is in all of this, so, "fear not." (Matt 1:20, NIV)

The shepherds are told that the gift of the Messiah is for them, so they need not be, as only the King James Version can describe, "sore afraid." (Luke 2:10)

In each of these instances, we can infer that the angel of the Lord is an awesome spectacle to behold. Something is scary. God is asking for trust. Trust in the face of fear. For each player in this Christmas pageant, there is reason to be afraid, but God is there.

Today, there are people in the community and the church (maybe more so in the church). Who are afraid to love and welcome those who are different? Those who carry a label of disability or exhibit behaviors not in keeping with the expected social norms. Yes, reaching out to the unknown is scary. Reaching into the life of someone different is frightening.

When Mandy and I entered the foster care process the first time, we were scared. We knew it was the right thing, but we were unprepared for this reality. Even when we received the phone call that we were being matched, we were scared. Like Zacharias, knowing that our prayers had been heard, was maybe more terrifying. "Why would God trust us with this?" It was not because "God only gives special kids to special people," for nearly all parents of children labeled with disabilities know this to be garbage. Rather, like Mary herself proclaimed, we learned that God was letting us know that "nothing is impossible for God." It was not about us (our specialness or lack of). It was about God and His glory alone. *soli deo gloria.*

Each time we have been fearful in our journey. A cancer diagnosis. Embarking on a new journey in foster care and adoption. Regardless of the point we are at, we have a choice at each point in the journey to listen to the fear and allow that to define us, or to acknowledge the fear and pray, like Elisha did, to open our eyes so that we more clearly see God in this. The writer of Deuteronomy proclaims: *"Be strong and courageous, do not be afraid or tremble at them, for the Lord your God is the one who goes with you. He will not fail you or forsake you."* (Deuteronomy 31:6, NIV) Summer teaches me regularly to be strong and courageous and reminds me that the Lord my God goes with, AND He does NOT fail or forsake us. Amen

Fear Not: Now What?

I find that to be a fool as to worldly wisdom, and to commit my cause to
God, not fearing to offend men, who take offence at the simplicity of
truth, is the only way to remain unmoved at the sentiments of others.-
John Woolman[26]

As people in the U.S. entered a state of quarantine and isolation because of COVID-19, the fear associated was palpable. Health, finances, relationships and more now felt unpredictable. This was new. This was unpredictable. This was uncomfortable. This was unplanned. Embracing the unknown causes fear and trepidation in many.

Following God's call in our lives often presents similar feelings. Choosing to foster or adopt is new, unpredictable, and often uncomfortable. Living life with a child labeled with disabilities or chronic illness is not planned, but it is unpredictable and, again, often uncomfortable. As well, living in a relationship with a child labeled with disabilities or with chronic illness can feel isolating.

While some families have embraced the unknown through foster or adoption and some other have embraced the unknown of life with disability, including the fears of health rationing, IEPs, living options, and career options. These families take each day one step at a time. Yet, many of us feel the isolation that stems from the mere

---

[26] Woolman, J., & Whittier, J. G. (1900). *The Journal of John Woolman: With an Introduction by John Greenleaf Whittier.* Headley brothers.

fact that many others are afraid to enter a relationship with children, our loved ones, ourselves because of fear. The perceived *dfferent- ness* commonly associated with children brought up in the foster sys- tem, or with adopted children, or with individuals labeled with disa- bilities too often serves as a barrier that many are too afraid to cross.

Henri Nouwen left academia to spend time amongst those with disabilities. During this time, he met a young man named Adam, a young man with cognitive disabilities who was also non-verbal. Nouwen would spend a considerable amount of time working and learning from Adam. This work resulted in the book aptly titled, *Ad- am*[27]. Nouwen's provides insights into the work of grace and com- passion as seen in the life of Adam, and the need to remove the fear of letting go of the comfortable in order to embrace the adventure God has in store. These insights have influenced me from my first introduction as a young undergraduate in San Diego to the present day.

EMBRACE THE MESSAGE

Nouwen says that "Adam was—very simply, quietly, and uniquely—there! He was a person, who by his very life announced the marvelous mystery of our God: I am precious, beloved, whole, and born of God." The idea that Adam was not an object of fear, but

---

[27] Nouwen, H. J. (2012). *Adam: God's beloved*. Orbis Books.

rather a living testimony who "bore silent witness" to the mystery of God is at the heart of this lesson. Adam, as are every single person labeled with differences, is worthy of relationship not because "he could speak, walk, or express himself, whether or not he made money, had a job, was fashionable, famous, married or single." In fact, Nouwen claims, "it had to do with his being." It had everything to do with the fact that "He was and is a beloved child of God."

We must see every single individual as an opportunity to give and receive the love of God. We must see every individual as an image bearer of God and a fellow recipient of God's grace. Fear leads us to demand proof. We want individuals to prove they are worth our time, attention, love, grace, etc. Yet, the message of grace reminds us that love drives out fear. It reminds us that "Life is a gift. Each one of us is unique, known by name, and loved by the One who fashioned us."

Unfortunately, as Nouwen points at, "there is a very loud, consistent, and powerful message coming to us from our world that leads us to believe that we must prove our belovedness by how we look, by what we have, and by what we can accomplish."

Yet, if we are to move beyond the fear that keeps us in isolation, the fear the marginalizes those who are different, the fear that God might not be enough, or the fear that the world's comforts are all we have to trust in, we must embrace the message that God is enough. We must embrace the message that God's grace is sufficient, even in our moment of fear. As Nouwen says, "We need to hear the message announced and see the message embodied, repeatedly. Only then do we find the courage to claim it and to live from it."

THEN TAKE A STEP

Once we embrace this message, then it is incumbent upon us to move. But where to? We move toward each other. If fears keep us from moving into relationship with the "other," then love (fears natural enemy) moves us into relationship. Maybe want to foster or adopt, but we are afraid of what it will cost in terms of money, relationships, time, and plans. Maybe we want to welcome the individual labeled with a disability into our group, relationship, or family, but we are afraid that we won't know what to say or that our priorities might have to shift. Maybe we are afraid of dropping our egos to build a home alongside those in need. Regardless of the rationalizations, it is fear that keeps us from doing the right thing, but it is love that will help us make the first step.

That first step requires to not only embrace the message but also discard the false trappings of the lie that we need more. That we need more than what God has provided and promises. For Nouwen, Adam's life stripped away that lie, not in some false-inspirational narrative, but in a real and meaningful way. As Nouwen describes it, "[Adam] seemed to be without concepts, plans, intentions, or aspirations. He was simply present, offering himself in peace and completely self-emptied so that the fruits of his ministry were pure and abundant." Adam's lack of pretense encouraged Nouwen to let go of his, which allowed them both to enter fearless relationship.

Yet, there is a first step that is required. A step of faith not fear. A step of love not fear. A choice to live in relationship not fearful distance. Taking that step led Nouwen to the truth that "the final significance of Adam's passion: a radical call to accept the truth of our lives and to choose to give our love when we are strong and to receive the love of others when we are weak, always with tranquility and generosity."

For some that first step is making small talk with the quirky newcomer. For others the first step is going to a foster/adoption information meeting. For others it is asking forgiveness from the person your ego has kept you from embracing. The great truth is that while the fear feels strong and while feels overwhelming, there is a God who IS love, and love conquers fear. To this point Nouwen writes on the passing of his friend Adam. "His mission is fulfilled. Yet it is not over. It will never be over, because love is stronger than fear and life is stronger than death. Adam's love and Adam's life are not meant for corruption. They are eternal because they are part of God's love and God's life." Amen.

Lesson #7: There is Beauty to Be Found

"Oh, my goodness!!" Summer shouted. "It's so beautiful, it made me cry a little bit." Summer and I had been driving just west of Interstate 5 in California. It was late at night and the sky was clear. The farmland, miles away from the Interstate, offered a perfect opportunity to gaze at the wonders of the stars. Summer looked out the window and laughed as she yelled out that she could see the big dipper, and the little dipper. She was so excited. "Isn't God amazing!?!" she asked in a knowing manner that directly speaks to her faith that God is. Yes, that God is. God exists. God is who He says He is. God loves Summer. God created a world in which she belongs.

In the beginning. This is how most of us learned the creation story. We repeat, "In the beginning God created the Heaven and the Earth." (Genesis 1:1, KJV) Yet we often forget about the chaos into which the voice of creation spoke. The Message says it this way, "First this: God created the Heavens and Earth—all you see, all you don't see. Earth was a soup of nothingness, a bottomless emptiness, an inky blackness." (Genesis 1:1, MSG) Regardless of the versions, there is a distinct understanding that chaos is not good, but God created something that was, in fact, good.

The void was also formless. Genesis 1:2 uses the Hebrew word *tohu,* which is traditionally translated as *formless.* The word can be translated as formless, but also as confusion, unreality, or emptiness. Yet it is into this chaos, confusion, unreality, and emptiness that God first speaks creation. This has always been an encouragement to me. Knowing that God is a God of cosmos, e.g. creation. God is a God of beauty amid the chaos.

I love camping with my family. A few years ago, the four of us were camping along the shores of Manzanita Lake in Lassen National Park. Mandy and Elijah had already gone to bed for the evening. Summer and I sat outside near the campfire. I asked her if she wanted to see something special. She did, so we walked along the lake away from the campsites. Without the obstruction of the trees or the lights from fellow campers, Summer could look up and see the beauty of the night sky. She wrapped her arms around me, gripping me tightly, and simply said, "thank you daddy."

Summer is grateful for the beauty of the stars. Nearly every time that we arrive home from an outing after dark, we experience the same routine. Mandy or I will say to the kids, "ok it's late, so let's make sure we do X, Y, or Z right away." They both agree on principle, but as soon as Summer walks out of the car she will look up into the night sky and immediately all other plans have been erased. She looks up and the stars are barely visible. This is not the beautiful sky of the national park or the bright sky of farmland. Yet, Summer will stand for what seems like hours (it's only a few moments) staring up. Toward the sky. She will call for both Mandy and I to join her as she stares up from the driveway. We, of course, are busy. We have what we imagine being, better things to do. Yet, Summer compels us to join her and look up. All she is asking is for us to take a moment out of our hectic suburban life and appreciate the stars. She wants us to revel in the same beauty that God pointed out to Abraham. She wants us to enjoy the same brilliance that God used as a message to those looking for the Christ child. When I take the briefest of moments to look up with Summer, I cannot help but to say, "thank you for sharing that with me Summer." I then give her a hug and we walk in the house with a smile on our faces. We are better for slowing down to share the beauty.

Sometimes that beauty is as present as the stars in the black of night. They shine against the black backdrop of the night. Yet sometimes those same stars struggle to be seen. The light pollution caused by highly populated areas limits our ability to clearly see the night sky. The stars are there, hidden behind the haze. The beauty is there to be found.

Summer continues to teach me this. However, I have not only learned that beauty is found all around me. More importantly, perhaps is the truth that the faster I go, the harder it is to see the beauty. It is difficult to notice anything of beauty on the fast-paced, congested freeways. It is once I get onto the slower roads that I can breathe it in. In fact, as I walk slowly through the world, I am more aware of the beauty to be found. Of course, I might also become more aware of the ugliness (for make no mistake there is ugliness in this world), but I miss the beauty amid the ugliness when I am rushing through life.

Summer is beautiful. Maybe I am biased, but I stand by my claim. I see her and recognize that she is beautiful. I also see my wife and recognize how beautiful she is. My response to my wife is reactive. She smiles and I smile. She walks into a room and my spirits are lifted. I find it fairly easy to recognize the beauty in my family, in my daughter, and in my wife. Yet, Summer isn't teaching me to recognize beauty as much as she is teaching me to seek it out. To slow down and turn my head. To take my time and breathe deeply of the "good" that God created. She is teaching me that though there is ugliness or chaos around me, therein lies the opportunity for something beautiful to begin.

Let me say here that I am not advocating that we make life miserable, so we learn a lesson. I am not advocating the "silver lining" school of thought regarding the difficulties of life. Rather, I argue that too often all I see is chaos because it is truly there. The chaos of abuse, isolation, are all genuine despair. These are not hidden from Summer. Rather, there is potential for beauty to speak Truth (with a capital T) into that chaos.

One of the great myths of American Christianity is that God makes life better. So, someone that was sick becomes better. Someone was not as pretty as they could be, so now they is prettier. We think of God's role in our lives as one of degree. That is not true at all. I am not saying that a relationship with God does not make life better, that is sometimes true. But more importantly, God is a God of opposites. In Chapter 61 of his book, the prophet Isaiah proclaims (I particularly like the language of the King James version here) that he has been anointed by God to proclaim the great exchange. God brings life from death. He brings creation from chaos and calls it good. He makes clean the unclean. He exchanges beauty for ashes, freedom for captivity, joy for mourning, garments of praise for the spirit of heaviness so "that He might be glorified." (Isaiah 61:3 KJV). This does not sound like a God that simply makes things better.

David Thoreau famously stated that "most men live lives of quiet desperation" simply trudging along. Some lives get better and some lives get worse, but the ho-hum of everyday existence is reality for most. God steps into this chaos and does something radically unexpected (even unexpected for many so-called believers). God makes the great exchange. The most remarkable is that God so loved this world that He gave His one and only son to stand in exchange for us.

Summer recognizes the exchanges. Maybe more so because her life has been filled with so much chaos and pain. Maybe she just has an innate ability to seek and find it. As I learn from her, I can see it more as well.

I recall one Christmas many years ago when my mom invited our entire family to one of those "Night in Bethlehem" walkthroughs at a local church. Before the Bethlehem tour, one of the volunteers gathered every in our group (there were 15 of us with my sisters and their families). The point of this walk through was to connect the Christmas story with the Easter story. The volunteer asked our group what we knew about the cross and grave. Summer boldly proclaimed, "Jesus died and on the third day He rose from the tumor."

You see, to her death, the tomb, and tumors are one and the same. She understood that her cancer could have meant death. In fact, it was through Cancer that she began to understand mortality. So, it made perfect sense for her to proclaim that when Christ defeated death, He also defeated tumors. To Summer, the story she tells of her life has cancer in it. However, there is a God who defeated tumors, who defeated death, who rose from the grave. Once again, she sees a Savior that did not simply make her life better, but one that through the cross and an empty tomb (or empty tumor) stood triumphant over death. She understands the great exchange, for as she will tell anyone willing to listen, "God saved my life."

I said earlier that all adoptions start with loss. This is part of the story. Adoption, however, when it comes together is a thing of beauty few can comprehend. Adoption doesn't make a life better; it is part of this great exchange. Paul references adoption in Galatian 4:5 insofar that he is reminding us that as part of the great heavenly we get to become children of God. This is not a program that makes our current father better, rather we exchange one inheritance and destiny with a completely different one.

So, while adoptions start with loss, we were lost until God made the exchange. They are a picture of the beauty to be found. Our adoption was no different. The family court building where our adoption was held is typically a place of chaos. It is a place where families are separated or where families are barely holding on. It is a place where the physical, sexual, emotional abuse of children finds its way into the court records. The hallways are littered with brokenness. I had been to family court many times before with boys and girls, hoping that this time mom or dad would show up ready to take them home, only to find that the judge has issued a continuance. So the young man or woman that I had driven to court would resignedly find their way back to the home or facility knowing that this building they had just left was a soul crushing, hope robbing institution set against them.

Yet on one bright Monday morning in June 2009, there was beauty to be found. Typically, the queue to enter family court was long. It would wrap around the building as all who entered had to be scanned and checked. No phones or cameras are allowed in the family court building. The sheriffs knew why most adults were there and rarely gave them the benefit of the doubt. Yet, on our appointed day, we were told "have someone from your party go to the front and tell one of the sheriff deputies that you are here for an adoption." So, that is exactly what I did.

"How many are with you?" the deputy asked. There was Mandy and I, my sister Kristen and her daughter Alex, my mom and dad, Mandy's mom, and some family friends.

"About ten," I replied.

"Ok, get them all together and bring them all up front here," he directed.

We did as instructed, then smiling, we were ushered in. They allowed us to keep our phones and cameras. Later, a deputy told me they loved escorting adoption groups in. He said to me, "typically this place is the worst, but seeing kids finally get connected with families never gets old."

As we entered the courtroom, everyone was smiling in great anticipation. The judge made some brief comments, then Mandy and I swore an oath. We committed to be responsible and caring. We promised our daughter in much the same way we had made a commitment nearly seven years prior before God, our family, and our friends. Then the judge brought down the gavel and Summer literally jumped for joy. Once the gavel came down, she traded in her old name for a new one. Sure, we all agreed that Summer would keep her "Summer," but she received a new middle name (Joy) and took on our family name. To this day, the site of my daughter cheering her adoption into a shared family with Mandy and I is one of the most beautiful things I have ever seen.

From the Family Archives (June 9, 2009)

So, it is all finally over. This long chapter in our lives that began many years ago has now come to an exciting conclusion. Monday morning, in front of our family and friends at the Orange County Family and Probate Court Building, Mandy and I raised our right hands and took an oath before the Judge that we would bear all the responsibilities of being a legal parent. The judge was great. He was fun and encouraging. The entire day was great.

I had been to that courthouse dozens of times with various foster youth, never once have I heard the court room clap at a pronouncement. Monday was special. Monday was different. It was the joyous culmination of a long, difficult process.

At the end of the day, as if on cue, Summer broke out into cheers. When she is excited, she shouts "TA-TA-TA-DA" at the top of her lungs with her head leaned back in Joy. As if the Lord hadn't provided enough confirmation, this was, yet again, another sign for Mandy and I of the goodness of God.

The judge said something profound at the end of the hearing, which I'll paraphrase now from my faith perspective: In a world that is fallen and broken, for a brief moment we could see traces of Heaven.

So that's it. Our adoption journey is over. This chapter in our lives is over and the next chapter has just started. We have been humbled by the countless individuals who have shared how our story has prompted them to become a foster parent or to adopt. We are blessed by the countless family members and friends who have prayerfully supported us through this journey. We look forward to their prayers and support in the years to come.

We are blessed by a loving and sovereign God who did what He does best: He takes Chaos and makes Cosmos. In the chaos of the foster care system, the chaos of abuse and neglect, the chaos of a broken world, God took the discordant sounds of it all and created the harmony of FAMILY. We are truly blessed.

A prolonged stay in a hospital is an exercise in drudgery. While Summer recovered on her hospital bed from her kidney removal surgery, Mandy and I watched and prayed. While Summer lay hooked up to wires and tubes, needles and tape we kept a vigil. Every hour some doctor making rounds, a surgeon following up, a nurse checking vitals would be in and out of our room. It felt like uncontrollable chaos. We had to rethink life. We were moving into the unknown. We were moving into the void, into the darkness that roamed the corridors of family court buildings of hospital waiting rooms. We were scared. We could practically feel the overwhelming weight of despair. Despite some meaningful friends and family, we could not help but to feel alone. In short, the time in the hospital felt like chaos.

Most nights, Mandy and I took turns watching over Summer. On alternate nights Mandy would sleep in the uncomfortable green 'parent" chair and I would go home. The next night we would trade. On the mornings following the nights in which I slept at home, I would show up at the hospital with coffee and a pastry for Mandy. Mandy would brief me on the comings and goings from the night before. I would then settle in with a book and take my turn with Summer. Without knowing it, Mandy and I were ships passing in the night. We debriefed each other, but we weren't connecting. We were entertaining visitors, who meant well, but demanded so much time and attention. We were exhausted, confused, and running on empty. Then in the midst of the darkness there came something beautiful. There was a light in that dark time.

My sister Kristen understands the needs of those walking through the void. Walking through chaos. One night, after about a week of Mandy not connecting, Kristen showed up in our hospital room with a back of groceries and a book. She told us to go across the street to the mall and have a date night.

We are thankful for each visitor who came to visit Summer. We are thankful for every free meal and gift card (again, never undervalue the gift of food). Yet these kindnesses could be a little exhausting at times. Kristen came into our room and gave us the gift of time, the gift of each other. She stepped into our chaos and filled the void with beauty. Yes, beauty. Thoughtful gifts done in selfless ways are beautiful.

On that first night, we walked over to Main Place Mall in Santa Ana, which sits directly across the street from the Children's Hospital. I cannot even remember where we ate. It did not matter. I could just look at my wife. She could look at me. We could simply be. Kristen would continue to do this once or twice a week while we were in the hospital. But that's not all. Once Summer came home and our lives entered a new routine, I went back to work. Meanwhile, Mandy's routine was tough as she was directed not to take Summer out of the house (spoiler alert: we didn't always comply). Even into this "inky blackness" my sister Kristen showed up once or twice a week and told Mandy, "Go out, do whatever, I've got this." By that time Mandy had found out that she was pregnant, so the gift of time continued to prove to be beautiful. The movement of God as He crafts something "good" out of chaos is beautiful.

Famed atheist Richard Dawkins declared that the universe "has precisely the properties we should expect if there is, at bottom, no design, no purpose, no evil, no good, nothing but blind, pitiless indifference."[28] Maybe, from a particular point of view, he has a point. There are people living in quiet desperation. There are people

---

[28] Dawkins, R. (2008). *River out of Eden: A Darwinian view of life*. Basic books.

living in pitiless indifference. But there is beauty, there is good, there is light. There is something to this whole creation. There is something that tells that this evil and pitiless indifference is wrong. Why would we argue that it is wrong if we did not also recognize a "right?" C.S. Lewis, in *Mere Christianity,* stated that his

> *"argument against God was that the universe seemed so cruel and unjust. But how had I got this idea of just and unjust? A man does not call a line crooked unless he has some idea of a straight line. What was I comparing this universe with when I called it unjust...? Of course, I could have given up my idea of justice by saying it was nothing but a private idea of my own. But if I did that, then my argument against God collapsed too – for the argument depended on saying that the world was really unjust, not simply that it did not happen to please my private fancies. Thus in the very act of trying to prove that God did not exist – in other words, that the whole of reality was senseless – I found I was forced to assume that one part of reality – namely my idea of justice – was full of sense. Consequently, atheism turns out to be too simple."* [29]

My argument is far less profound than Lewis, however. I have seen great suffering. I have railed against a God that allowed my daughter to suffer abuse, to face great illness, and to face the pitiless indifference of a world that has little room for people who are different. Yet, if you ask me about Summer's biological mother and her choices or were to ask me if I would rather things were different, I don't know what I would say. I now have faith that God's perspective is far better than mine. I also know that if the beauty and light

---

[29] Lewis, C. S. (2001). *Mere Christianity.* Zondervan. Grand Rapids, MI.

that I have seen as a result are even just the smallest glimpse of a world to come, then. . . 1) I am so excited for what is coming. 2) If it meant missing out on the moments of light and beauty, then I would not change a thing. Maybe that's a weak answer, but, the manner in which Summer's story has taught me to look, to seek deeply, the beauty and light in my story is a welcome respite in this world and leaves me longing for the world to come.

In the *Magician's Nephew*, C. S. Lewis tells of the creation of the land of Narnia by the great Aslan. On the same trip to Lassen National Park, our family listened to the audio versions of each book in the Chronicles of Narnia series. Maybe I had forgotten the power of these stories, or maybe my life positioned me to hear the words with new ears. Regardless of the reasons, as I heard Aslan sing Narnia into creation, I was moved deeply in my soul. I will close with the scene in which Digory (the Magician's Nephew) heard the notes and bore witness to the beauty a creator can bring from darkness.

> *In the darkness something was happening at last. A voice had begun to sing... it seemed to come from all directions at once... Its lower notes were deep enough to be the voice of the earth herself. There were no words. There was hardly even a tune. But it was beyond comparison, the most beautiful noise he had ever heard. It was so beautiful Digory could hardly bear it.* [30]

---

[30] Lewis, C. S. (2005). *The Magician's Nephew*. Zondervan. Grand Rapids, MI.

There is beauty to be found: Now What?

When God is involved, anything can happen. Be open. Stay that way. God has a beautiful way of bringing good vibrations out of broken chords. -Charles Swindoll

---

As Jesus calls the first disciples, the gospel of John recounts an exchange between Phillip and Nathaniel. *"Philip found Nathanael and said to him, "We have found Him of whom Moses in the Law and also the Prophets wrote—Jesus of Nazareth, the son of Joseph." Nathanael said to him, "Can any good thing come out of Nazareth?" Philip said to him, "Come and see." (John 1:45-46, NASB)* Nathaniel (as do others in John's gospel see John 7:41-42 and John 7:52) gives voice to something many of us think yet keep to ourselves. Namely, the things of God, the beautiful things, the precious gifts, the true joys only come to us when they check all the boxes or meet the preposterous standards, we have set for them. Yet Phillip's response is the response I desperately want in my own life. It is the response my daughter gives when I am dubious of her wonder, and it is the same response given by the Woman at the Well (see John chapter 4) . . .Come and See.

"Come and see," it is the request, no, it is the demand, of every child who has found their great treasure of discovery and compels others to share in the joy that stems from the beauty. As I learn to find the beauty, I am blessed to receive these glimpses of heaven. Hope is offered in that simple invitation-Come and See. I find joy when I accept that invitation to look for the beauty. Joy, though, is not an appreciation of aesthetic characteristics. Rather it comes when the deep longings of my heart are met with the deep love of a savior who, according to Paul, "does not disappoint." (Romans 5:5, NASB)

Paul speaks further of beauty that brings joy in his letter to the Roman where he quotes the prophet Isaiah who says, "And how can anyone preach unless they are sent? As it is written: "How beautiful are the feet of those who bring good news!" (Romans 10:15, NIV, see also Isaiah 52:7) This I continue to learn. My daughter is beautiful in every way, but most importantly because she brings forth the good news of Jesus into the world. Unfortunately, too few expect the many contributions and gifts of Summer and others who have been sidelined by our culture, both religious and secular. As a result, these low expectations prevent those in positions of power and privilege from seeking out those beautiful gifts. Consequently, we fail to celebrate the contributions from those who could bring so much more than mainstream culture allows.

EXPECT IT

C.S. Lewis, among other topics, wrote prodigiously on Joy. He distinguishes between mere happiness over something pretty or nice and the genuine joy that comes from the deeper longings of our hearts. He writes, "Joy is distinct not only from pleasure in general but even from aesthetic pleasure. It must have the stab, the pang, the inconsolable longing."[31] In other words, true Joy is longed for. It is expected. Too often, individuals labeled with disabilities have so few expectations of what they can do, that few ever find the beauty and the joy of their fellowship. As I have lived life alongside Summer, I have learned to lean into the phrase "come and see" as I have grown to expect. I have learned that my preconceptions are not a match for God's work in this world.

Again, this is why Mandy and I gave Summer the middle name, Joy. Summer's advent into our life spoke to our deeper longings and the fulfillment of that longing. Summer Joy's entrance was beautiful. While we expected her arrival, we were unprepared for what God did in our lives. Yet, if we had no expectation that there was beauty and joy to be found along this difficult journey, we would have missed out on so much. This truth confirms again Lewis' thoughts on Joy. He wrote, "All Joy reminds. It is never a possession, always a desire for something longer ago or further away or still "about to be."

SEEK IT

In Romans chapter 12, Paul speaks to the essential parts of the body and the various gifts within that body. When we seek those gifts, because we expect them, we are taking part in a divine activity. The gifts those on the sidelines offer are of greater value than those things we mistake for beauty or even joy. Here Lewis

---

[31] Lewis, C. S. (1956). *Surprised by joy: The shape of my early life*. Houghton Mifflin Harcourt.

speaks from his own story. "Joy itself," he writes, "considered simply as an event in my own mind, turned out to be of no value at all. All the value lay in that of which Joy was the desiring. And that object, quite clearly, was no state of my own mind or body at all." This personal insight speaks both to the joy of expectation, but also the need to seek. More importantly, this need to seek is the seeking Jesus calls us to. It is the seeking of the Kingdom of God first, not the kingdom, gifts, and pleasures of the American dream, or, sad to say, even the American church.

CELEBRATE IT

The beauty and joy that I have learned to both expect and seek points me to something greater. It directs me to a Savior-Creator. It directs me to long for a world beyond this. It directs my attention away from the false pleasures of this world and toward the eternal. The desire for anything less than pure beauty and joy found in God, Lewis reminds us, "if idolatrously mistaken for Joy itself, soon honestly confessed themselves inadequate."

My daughter has taught me that the simple joys or the simple beauties in life are sign posts toward something greater. Because of that, I am learning to celebrate both the gifts as well as the one who brings them to my attention and my life. As Lewis again writes, "[joy] is a by-product. Its very existence presupposes that you desire not it but something other and outer."

Because this joy of the Lord brings me a larger perspective, I need to celebrate. My need to celebrate others, even when the world refuses to acknowledge, is my way of declaring that my hope, my expectations, have come true. That God has been faithful. My need to celebrate is my way of saying that the gifts of God are worth seeking, even when the seeking is in unexpected places. Ultimately, this celebration of beauty and joy, as well as the giver and the messenger, serve as signposts to something more, to somewhere more. Lewis says that joy serves as "a pointer to something other and outer." He says that even in times of darkness or fear, "the pointer naturally loomed large in [Lewis'] thoughts." He describes being lost in the woods and catching sight of a signpost that points the way toward the right path. I celebrate the beauty. I celebrate the joy. I celebrate the messenger. I celebrate because they are but markers, signs, and reminders that there is more, much more, overwhelmingly more to come.

Lesson #8: The things of God are ALWAYS worth the wait

"Am I a dream come true? Was I worth the wait?" Summer likes to ask. She knows the answer to these questions. In fact, when she first came to live with us, she had two t-shirts that she loved to wear. The first read, "I am a dream come true." The second read, "I was worth the wait." Summer asks those questions because she knows the answers. She asks the questions because it makes her happy to hear her story.

Some adoptive parents change a child's first, middle, and last name upon a successful adoption. There are great reasons for that. There are also arguments for keeping a name. At three and half years of age, Summer was already used to responding to her name. She looked when her name was called and connected a deeper meaning to the name Summer. Mandy and I knew that we could not disrupt that. Afterall, we could not change her name until after the adoption was finalized, which took a little over seven months to complete. So, after seven months of calling her Summer, we knew that the name was going to stick.

Yet, we had never called her by her middle or last name during that time, so we felt confident in altering those two. She took on our last name because she was joining our family. Mandy and I wrestled with her middle name. We wanted to make it an extension of our journey. Eventually we settled on "Joy."

Sure, Summer made us happy, but Joy expresses something deeper. It connects to waiting and to anticipation. More importantly, it connects to fulfillment. People too often seek happiness. We often try to make our kids, spouse, family, and friends happy. As believers, we serve a savior who brought Joy to the World. Happiness is happenstance, something fortuitous that causes momentary pleasure. Joy happens when the deep (often unknown) longing of our soul meets Holy fulfillment. One is momentary, the other transcends time. One is sensory, the other is spiritual. This is the lesson Summer brought to our lives. Through foster care, through adoption, through cancer, and considering her diagnosis. There is hope in the waiting. There is hope in the slow march of our lives. Most importantly, we learn that the things of God are always worth the wait.

From the Family Archives (Christmas 2008)

There is nothing quite like Christmas time. There is no other time of the year that I enjoy more. I am one of those people who look forward every year to that moment when radio stations begin playing Christmas music. I am not of the opinion that Christmas music comes too soon. (In fact, I question how anyone can be opposed to radio stations that stop playing songs about casual love, one-night-stands, or simple hedonism and begin playing songs that glorify virginity, peace, joy and the birth of Christ.) There are so many elements of this season that resonate for me. The scene at the Manger, the annunciation, the visit of the magi, the star, the flight to Egypt as well as candy canes, carols, gifts and yes, Virginia, Santa Claus all make this season meaningful, year in and year out.

This year is especially meaningful for Mandy and I. When we started our adoption process in 2006, we hoped to have a little one grace our home by last Christmas. This didn't happen. We bought a stocking, hung it beside ours and prayed that another Christmas would not go by before a child entered our home. This Christmas we will fill that stocking for our little girl, we will include her in family traditions from the spiritual to the quirky. We will tell her about a God who loved her so much that He sent His only Son as a gift to all.

As I reflect on Christmas this year, I am reminded of Simeon the Priest. This is a man that doesn't get a lot of attention at Christmas, but deserves so much. Simeon was an older man, but God had promised him that he would not die until he saw the Messiah. Imagine, year after year of waiting. Imagine the anticipation, the nervous excitement as children were brought to him for blessing. I wonder if he saw the parents coming for a dedication and got excited thinking that this could be the one. I also wonder if he felt a little depressed as each family left, knowing he still had to wait. Yet, Simeon knew that God is a keeper of promises and does not have people wait in vain. So, everyday Simeon went to the temple expecting God to, well, be God. I can only imagine the JOY Simeon felt as Mary and Joseph approached. He must have been beside himself with JOY.

Simeon was undoubtedly old and weary of the wait. He must have desperately wanted to let slip this mortal coil and now he was holding God's promise fulfilled. "God, you can now release your servant; release me in peace as you promised. With my own eyes I've seen your salvation; it's now out in the open for everyone to see." (Luke 1:32 MSG)

We understand a little of the waiting as well as the JOY at a promise fulfilled. Even though she can't articulate it, we believe our daughter feels the same way. For 3 ½ years she has waited for the promise of a family. Foster parents, social workers, therapists, volunteers and staff came and went, but none of them were the promise fulfilled. It must have been confusing and tiresome. Every ounce of her being must have yearned for the waiting to be over and for God to provide her with a family. Yet, she never let these situations rob her of her JOY and infectious good spirit. We believe she gets the point of family. She refers to us as "mommy" and "daddy" (something she has never referred to staff or other foster parents as). She refers to her home as "my home." She refers to our family as "family." Even though none of us knew it at the time, we have all three been waiting for each other and God brought us together at just the right time.

We also believe that she gets the point of Christmas. This was proved the other day as we were getting ready for Church. Mandy said to her, "It's time for Church." She looked at Mandy and said, "ch-u-ch." Then she said, "Baby Yeesus?" She then walked over to our little nativity set and picked up the baby Jesus and gave Him a hug. Yeah, she gets it.

One final thought: When Gabriel tells Mary that she is going to have a child. Mary is a bit astonished and asks Gabriel how something so wonderful can happen. Gabriel looks at her and replies that nothing is too wonderful for God (some translations have nothing is impossible, Luke 1:37). We are aware of the truth of this passage, as Mandy and I often wonder if this is all too good to be true or if our little girl is too wonderful. In a season of hope and peace, it is easy to forget that nothing is too wonderful for God. As people ready themselves for New Year's resolutions, goals and plans, it is easy to forget that nothing is too wonderful for God. We know that many people are finding it hard to hold onto that truth this year. We know that finances make planning for the next year difficult. We know that many people are hurting with the loss of a loved one. We know that hundreds of thousands of foster children are waiting for the promise of a family. We know that families are waiting for the promise of a child. Around the world, we know that millions are waiting for their forever family. We know that relationships don't always work out the way we hope. However, our Christmas prayer is that you too will find the truth of God's promises in this Holiday season. Remember that peace and hope can still be found. Remember that the story of Christmas is not about the magi's gifts to Christ as much as the gift of Christ. Remember that miracles still happen and that nothing, absolutely nothing, is too wonderful for God.

In the early 1970s two Princeton Psychologists, John Darley and C. Daniel Batson, looked at the parable of the Good Samaritan. In short, they asked a group of Seminary students to deliver a sermon on the well-known parable of the Good Samaritan as found in Luke 10:25-37. The student-subjects were asked to give the sermon in a building across campus and told that they would be graded by their academic advisors/supervisors.[32]

Batson and Darley were interested in how time constraints and pressures would impact their supposed, helpful nature, or compassion. After all, the students were being trained to become ordained priests, so it was a safe hypothesis to presume that they were inclined to help others.

As each student finished their preparation, Batson and Darley imposed elements of time constraint upon them by giving them one of three instructions:

- "You're late. They were expecting you a few minutes ago... You'd better hurry. It shouldn't take but just a minute." This was the high-hurry condition.
- "The (studio) assistant is ready for you, so please go right over." This was the intermediate-hurry condition.
- "It'll be a few minutes before they're ready for you, but you might as well head on over. If you have to wait over there, it shouldn't be long.' This was the low-hurry condition.

Upon receiving the time-constraint the students walked toward the other side of the campus. During the walk to the other side of the campus, each student encountered a 'victim' in a deserted alleyway

---

[32] Darley, J. M. & Batson, C. D. (1973). " From Jerusalem to Jericho": A study of situational and dispositional variables in helping behavior. *Journal of personality and social psychology, 27*(1), 100.

just like the wounded traveler in the parable of the Good Samaritan. This victim (an associate of the experimenters) appeared destitute, was slouched and coughing and clearly in need of assistance. The seminarians were thus offered a chance to apply what they were about to preach.

Batson and Darley wanted to know if time pressure affected the seminarians' response to a person in need. Sadly, though probably not too surprising, only 10% of the students in the high-hurry situation stopped to help the person in need. 45% of the students in the intermediate-hurry and 63% of the students in the low-hurry situations helped the person in need.

The authors concluded that "A person not in a hurry may stop and help a person in distress. A person in a hurry is likely to keep going. Ironically, he is likely to keep going even if he is hurrying to speak on the parable of the Good Samaritan, thus inadvertently confirming the point of the parable... Thinking about the Good Samaritan did not increase helping behavior, but being in a hurry decreased it." In short, HURRYING PREVENTS HELPING.

It is sad to think the knowledge of the Word of God, which we can assume these Seminaries had in abundance, had less impact on their Christian charity than the clock. Maybe this is why I received the following in an email from the high school pastor at our church to inform me that his staff's schedule is too full to find space for Summer: "Additionally, I know we had talked about having our youth team trained, so that we can be better equipped to minister to students with autism [but] at this moment our schedule is pretty packed. I can be in touch with you at a future date though, to revisit the opportunity for our youth team to be trained."

This pastor does not mean to offend. He does not differ from the seminarians fifty years ago. He has pressures and deadlines, schedules and commitments. Yet, I have a daughter who takes a while to get things. Who does things a few steps slower than her peers. Who reaches developmental milestones at her own pace. My daughter desperately needs someone to gift her their time. If they do, I am convinced that it will be time well spent.

The literature on inclusion and belonging shows that it is one thing to be included, yet it is something else entirely to be wanted. The pull to be wanted, to be involved, and to connect transcends ability. We demonstrate that another is wanted by creating space, both physically and temporally, for that individual. Therefore, the fact that many local churches implicitly, and occasionally explicitly, argue that *all individuals are wanted as long as they fit into the schedule*, creates a major barrier to belonging. Theologian John Swinton in *Becoming Friends of Time: Disability, Timefullness, and Gentle Discipleship* simply and clearly asserts that "[t]hose who are made in God's image have time for one another."

Time. We are all equally blessed with the same number of hours in our day. Yet how we spend our time is such a telling indicator of our values. When you ask a friend to get together for coffee and they tell you they are "too busy." We typically, and more often than not, accurately, hear, "I am too busy for you." That person's time is allocated to "more important things." When we refer to someone as being on the margins, we mean that they do not have influence, or prestige. We are arguing that they are not valued by modern society. In other words, we are saying that they are not worth the time. Sure we will stand in line to meet a celebrity or feel it is appropriate for a church to allow professional athletes or reality television stars to take the stage, but have that same pastor bring to the stage someone who does not fit our vision of a valued person take the stage and immediately the mutterings of "waste of time," can be heard.

One thing that amazes me about the ministry of Jesus is that He always had time. He had time to dine with Zacchaeus (Luke 19-1:10); He had time for the children (Matthew 19:14), despite the disciples' protest that they might be wasting Jesus' time, He had time for the Woman at the Well (John 4:4-26), for the woman with condition of blood (Luke 8:43-48), and for countless individuals the religious rulers of the day, and, too often, His own disciples, did not find time for. Each time Jesus takes time to talk, or eat and drink, or heal those who are not valued by the privileged elite of His day, He shows how to communicate a desire for belonging.

Jesus explicitly creates a space in which to invite the other into a belonging far better than they are currently experiencing. The belonging Jesus offers is squarely balanced on the fact that the individuals Jesus calls are wanted, that communion is wanted, that fellowship is wanted, and they are important enough for Jesus (the creator of time) to find time. Perhaps most telling, the belonging Jesus offers does so in full awareness that they are wanted because of who Jesus is, not because of what they offer. A faith-communities that reaches out and shows a desire for fellowship, without condition, embodies the belonging seen in the Gospel.

In an address to seminary students in 2015, John Swinton argued that Jesus did not "hangout" with the marginalized people such as Zacchaeus or the Woman at the Well. Rather, His gift of time and relational space completely changed the dynamics. Swinton argues that we wrongly talk about people being marginalized. Yes, certain people have been placed at the margins of existing power structures. People with disabilities like Summer are told they don't belong, or there is not enough time for them. Yet, Jesus, by creating a space for those rejected or seen as unworthy of attention, completely realigns the margins. Now those in power, the religious leaders and such, are now on the margins. The Good News of the Kingdom of God is being preached to shepherds on the hills, to sinners, tax collectors, and harlots. The Good News is available to the outcast and the leper, to the stranger and the stigmatized, to the prodigal children and to you and me. Now Theologian John Swinton claims that *"God was with a totally different group of people doing something quite different: offering friendship and acceptance and revealing the kingdom in and through that friendship."* This is a radical idea, in that Jesus *"offered relational space and time to people for whom the world had no time. In and through his friendships, he gave people back their names."*[33] You see, they were no longer nameless "so and so's." My daughter, in Jesus' presence, is no longer that "disruptive kid with autism." Rather she is Summer Joy, a child of God. She is known completely and loved unconditionally. That is what it means to be given back your name.

For people like Summer, too many congregations, from their point of view, simply do not have time. Yet, it is in this very gifting of time in which the great evangelists of the gospels speak. Zacchaeus, the Woman at the Well, the Blind Man, whoever Jesus stops to give the gift of time to, become His most ardent proclaimers. Jesus is not one who wastes time. Jesus is a creator of time. The way He gifts it, and to whom, should be instructional for our own lives.

---

[33] Swinton, J. (2015). Time, hospitality and belonging: Towards a practical theology of mental health. *Word & World*, 35(1), 171-181.

Even communities who want to include are often in a hurry to do so. John Swinton reminds us again that the ability to accomplish many things, including the creation of an inclusive community, is not the hallmark of the Christian community. Rather, he says, "[i]t is the ability to love, not the ability to include or tolerate, that is the primary mark of discipleship." The welcome that leads to belonging must begin with and end with love. For "[t]he vocation of the Christian community is to learn to love God, and in coming to love God, learn what it means to love and to receive love from all of its members."

Here I am reminded of the wisdom of my wife and a lesson she learned from her Sunday School days, "love is spelled T-I-M-E." God created time. God has gifted us with time. Those who do not fit into society's norms often require a bit more time. I wonder why too often we in the church, particularly the Western Church, are so stingy with our time.

Yet even I forget this. I am often so caught up in "being on time" or "staying on schedule" that Summer's slow pace is frustrating. Yet, Summer is constantly teaching me that her pace is the preferred pace. As she slowly walks through life, she sees things that I do not. In my hurry to "keep up" I am missing things. Her life is a signpost asking me to slow down. What God has in store for me is worth the wait, and I must slow down to see it.

Keep up. It is an interesting phrase. When I am keeping up with the world I am working at a frenetic pace rushing to accumulate. I am adding quasi-friends in a virtual world so I can rapidly scroll through their lives. I am "touching base" with people I purport to care about as I leave to make the next appointment. I am a tourist in the lives of the ones I claim to value. I am seeing what is there, so I remain informed, but I am too hurried to settle down and take up residence in their lives.

Yet, when I keep pace with Summer, I have no choice but to settle into her life. She points out the stars, the flowers, the lady-bugs, and so much more. When I keep pace with her, I cannot simply nod, smile, say, "that's nice," and move on. Rather, she demands that I look, that I engage, that I spend time. When I do, I realize that I have been missing the important things. I realize that my time has been poorly spent. I realize that when I compare her pace, my pace, and the pace of Jesus, she is much more in step with the pace of Jesus. She has time to notice the lilies of the field and the birds of the air. She always has time for a hug, no matter who is in line behind her or how emphatically others tell her to hurry along. Her pace stands in stark contrast to the world's race to accumulate money, power, influence, likes, or prestige. So, while she takes her time getting where she goes, it is always worth the wait.

In what has now become a graduation staple *Oh, The Places You'll Go*, the late, and great, Theodore Geisel, better known as Dr. Seuss, put his finger squarely on the issue with waiting. He wrote with enthusiasm about all the places you can and will go. But he understood that "bang-ups and hang-ups" would happen to us all. He understood that we all find ourselves in *Slumps*. He rightly noted that "unslumping" is not easily done. Yet, what I find most poignant is his ability to identify the *Waiting Place*. He wrote:

> *You can get so confused that you'll start in to race*
>
> *down long wiggled roads at a break-necking pace*

and grind on for miles cross weirdish wild space,

headed, I fear, toward a most useless place.

The Waiting Place...

...for people just waiting.

Waiting for a train to go

or a bus to come, or a plane to go

or the mail to come, or the rain to go

or the phone to ring, or the snow to snow

or the waiting around for a Yes or No

or waiting for their hair to grow.

Everyone is just waiting.

Waiting for the fish to bite

or waiting for the wind to fly a kite

or waiting around for Friday night

or waiting, perhaps, for their Uncle Jake

or a pot to boil, or a Better Break

or a string of pearls, or a pair of pants

or a wig with curls, or Another Chance.

Everyone is just waiting.

NO! That's not for you!

Somehow you'll escape

all that waiting and staying.

You'll find the bright places

where Boom Bands are playing. [34]

Every time I read this, I wonder how much of St. Paul's letter to the Romans Dr. Seuss was familiar with. This is the promise that I started off this book with.

Paul writes in Romans 5:3-5 (MSG) that, "[t]here's more to come: We continue to shout our praise even when we're hemmed in with troubles, because we know how troubles can develop passionate patience in us, and how that patience in turn forges the tempered steel of virtue, keeping us alert for whatever God will do next. In alert expectancy such as this, we're never left feeling shortchanged." This alert expectancy is a different waiting. It speaks to a waiting knowing that God does not disappoint. It speaks to a waiting that is always, always worth the wait. Paul continues, "[q]uite the contrary—we can't round up enough containers to hold everything God generously pours into our lives through the Holy Spirit!" It is as if I can almost see the Bright places. I can almost hear the Boom Band playing. Yet here is the biggest difference. When I wait on God, I need not escape. God generously brings the Bright Places, and the Boom Bands to me.

When Summer came to live with us it filled us with wonder and joy. Yet, it also filled us with anxiety and fear. Yes, Summer was

---

[34] Geisel, T. S. (1990). *Oh, the places you'll go!*. Random House Books for Young Readers.

definitely "worth the wait." She was (and is) a "dream come true." However, we could not always see it.

Bringing a child from the foster care system into your home has unique challenges. For a child who has not received the foundation of a safe and stable childhood, there is fear and anxiety that comes with that child. One approach to this "developmental trauma" is an intervention developed by Karen Purvis, a researcher at Texas Christian University's Institute of Child Development, known as Trust-Based Relational Intervention (TBRI).[35] TBRI has three core principles that aid in the establishment of trust: Empowerment (attention to physical needs), Connection (attention to attachment needs), and Correction (attention to behavioral needs).

These principles help both caregiver and child learn healthy ways of interacting, so both can play a role in the healing process. The challenge, however, is that these principles take time. When a family fosters or adopts, there has been a loss (see chapter 1). That loss takes time to heal. TBRI is a means for remediating that loss, but it takes time. Did I already say that? Well, good, because it does.

This is something that might come as a shock to those who live by Beatles' lyrics in their approach to thinking about (someone else's) foster and/or adopted youth. . ."all you need is love." Well, to paraphrase my wife's Sunday School expression, sometimes love expresses itself in time. This was true for us.

During the first six months, or so, of our time with Summer, we struggled. Summer was happy and loving, but sleep was a strug-

---

[35] Purvis, K. B., Cross, D. R., Dansereau, D. F., & Parris, S. R. (2013) Trust-Based Relational Intervention (TBRI): A Systemic Approach to Complex Developmental Trauma, *Child & Youth Services,* 34:4.

gle. She would not allow us to leave without going through an elabo-
rate routine. Even then, she would crawl out of bed and demand that
we hold her and rock her to sleep, sometimes until one or two in the
morning. Other nights, the only way we could get her to sleep was to
drive her around for an hour or more. This put a strain on Mandy
and my ability to connect in a way that we did not experience when
Elijah was born.

The weariness took its toll. When she was tired or uncomfortable, she would become aggressive. Other times she would spon-
taneously attempt to run away. We had to install locks at the top of
our apartment door, so she would not run into the street. We were
also quickly learning that she was one of the fastest, and strongest,
three and half years old either of us ever met.

But we had time. We gave her time. And over time she
trusted. She responded. All I can say is that sometimes we were not
sure we were going to get through it. We were not able to talk to
family and friends about our struggle, because they just did not understand. But God is faithful. We waited on the Lord and He gave
our family rest (albeit it seemed short once we got the cancer diagnosis, but that is for a different place). So, yes, Summer was worth
the wait. In fact, she will now over twelve years later, occasionally,
look at me and ask, "daddy, was I worth the wait?"

All I can do is look at her and smile (and try not to cry),
"yes, absolutely, you were and ARE worth the wait."

The things of God are ALWAYS worth the wait: Now What?

I wait for the Lord, my whole being waits, and in His word I put my hope.

-Psalm 130:5 (NIV)

Our modern society is premised on a wealth of lies and half-truths. Two lies attempt to keep the vulnerable, the oppressed, the abandoned, and the disabled marginalized. The first is that meaning and individual value is exemplified through the frenetic race to accumulate: power, knowledge, position, prestige, etc. The second is that meaning and individual value are further premised on one's ability to promote and/or demonstrate these acquisitions. Those who do not race to accumulate or those who do not self-promote may be seen to have less worth or no worth at all. Unfortunately, this is true both in the larger society as well as within the local church. Yet, there is a response to this rush... slow down.

This is the lesson Summer teaches me daily. Perhaps this is the most important lesson she has taught me. I may not be the best student, but she has been a patient and kind teacher who brings this important lesson to me again and again. She continues to teach that the attention to a slower pace, to the waiting, makes it possible to live in relationship with children impacted by the child welfare system and individuals labeled with disabilities. Without the slower pace, without the waiting, relationships here would not be possible. This seems to be the lesson that brings all the other lessons together meaningfully and significantly.

The slow, deliberate life allows so much more value than the life in which I rush to accumulate. Compassion, for instance, takes time. When I am rushing here and there, I do not have the time needed to build a home alongside those living in pain. Rather, I would rush through life as a loss-tourist. There is a deliberate slow pace to the compassionate life. A pace that those who have been abused and marginalized require to be brought into community. A life spent in obedience to the clock would prevent the life I know God has called me to.

As I rush through life, as I refuse to wait on God, I show a lack of trust. I show trust in my savior when I wait. I show trust as I slow down to His gentle pace. Counting blessings requires a slow approach that runs counter to the anxious, frenetic pace. Counting my blessings requires me to stop, to pause, and to wait.

Welcome requires time. Welcome and rushing are not compatible. Nothing is more welcoming than one person says to another, "I have time for you." Because nothing is more important than extending the love of God to my fellow man.

However, the urgent tasks that I can easily accumulate through my work-a-day life can keep me from the friendships and relationships that are so important in much the same way that the thorns strangled the seed thrown by the wayside. I embrace these lessons and I remember that God is enough. When I remember that God is enough, I remember to slow down. I remember my pursuit of my dreams, even the hallowed "American Dream," encourages me to race after things and miss the opportunities that are only opened when I slow down.

When I take my time, I can see that those to whom God calls me are not to be feared. Just like Elisha's servant, I need not rush to panic. Rather, I can pray and wait to see how God will triumph. This is true also when it is fear that keeps me from embracing those who are different or most vulnerable. As I lean into the path God calls me, I know that as I am faithful to wait; He is faithful to lead.

Often, His lead reveals beauty I would have missed in my rushing. There is something to be said about "stopping to smell the roses." Summer's call for me to stop what I am doing, to stop what I had planned, to give up my pace for hers more often than not leads to see beauty both in her and the world that I would have otherwise missed.

At the heart of these lessons I have learned from my amazing daughter is the need for me to change my pace and to change my perspective. Yet, in our modern society, that is far easier said than done. Another individual who has helped me understand how to respond to the demands of this world is the humble seventeenth century monk born Nicholas Herman, but better known to history as Brother Lawrence. Lawrence famously claimed, "It is enough for me to pick up but a straw from the ground for the love of God." His life and thoughts were collected in a series of conversations and maxims passed down to us as *The Practice of the Presence of God*. [36] This book

---

[36] Lawrence, B. & de Beaufort, J. (1981). *The Practice of the Presence of God: Based on the Conversations, Letters, Ways and Spiritual Principles of Brother Lawrence, as well as on the Writings of Joseph De Beaufort*. Thomas Nelson.

has been a reminder to me of how to live in this world without while not being seduced by the frenzied rush the world too often demands. Year after year I go back to this simple text and am reminded of the beauty and importance of the slow and simple life. Also, I see a way in which to apply the simple life.

WALK LIKE JESUS

Brother Lawrence observed that people "invent means and methods of coming at God's love, they learn rules and set up devices to remind them of that love, and it seems like a world of trouble to bring oneself into the consciousness of God's presence." While so many of us set up rules it is so much more straightforward to follow Jesus. When I walk as Jesus walked, I recognize a few things:

1) Jesus was never in a hurry. He never seemed to be in a rush. Jesus' pace was one in which conversation could be had. His pace allowed for both intimacy and conversation. Yes, Jesus walked, as this was the preferred mode of transportation of the day. Yet, in His walk we see a model for a way to live, even in these modern times.

2) Jesus had time for everybody. When others tried to hold people back from Jesus' presence, He created space for those individuals. He had time for children when most during His day did not. He had time for sinners and tax collectors. His pace when healing or speaking seems so different from the hurried pace of our modern church services.

REMOVE THE WASTE

Our modern society has made a virtual religion out of minimalism and removing waste. Yet, too little attention has been given to those things, both physical and virtual, that distract from our ability to spend time and cultivate deep and meaningful relationships. While many of us would acknowledge the need to remove the waste in our lives, too few of us do. Instead, most continue to look for the next app or method or tool that will "fix" things. We are still not willing to slow down, we are seeking to do more with the time we have. Removing the waste is not designed to streamline our frenzy. Rather, it allows us to slow down and lean into essential things.

Brother Lawrence encourages us to "occupy ourselves entirely in knowing God." The focus on the next app, tool, or method is less important than a life centered on knowing God. In fact, we should be so invested in our relationship with God that we regard leaving His presence as "trifles and fooleries." Once we recognize the distractions for the waste that they are, we can focus on the good news so of the Gospel which requires the slower deliberate pace of relationship, or as Brother Lawrence once again notes, "How happy we would be if we could find the treasure of which the Gospel speaks; all else would be as nothing."

Yet, removing the waste is a challenge, particularly with the clutter that modern technology provides. I find it useful to apply a framework for adopting new technology (or any tool really) as provided by Author, Pastor, and Blogger Tim Challies in *The Next Story*.[37]

---

[37] Challies, T. (2011). *The next story: Life and faith after the digital explosion.* Zondervan.

- Why were you created?
  - Understanding the original purpose of a tool or technology helps us better see how this addition may begin to shape and change us.
- What problem are you designed to solve?
  - Adding new things randomly to our lives rarely results in deeper relationships or a slower pace. Rather, slowing down to ask the necessary questions allows for a closer examination of consequences (even ones that are unintended)
- What new problems will you bring?
  - Any new tool or technology brings unintended consequences. We can all admit that our smartphones, while a great tool, have had unforeseen consequences. Again, taking the time to test the unintended consequences (such as technology that prevents deeper relationships in lieu of superficial quasi-friendship) allows for that deeper relationship.
- What are you doing to my heart?
  - Finally, this question is vital. Yet, to answer this question we must step out of the frenzy to examine our hearts, to examine our motives, and to focus on the things of God instead of the "trifles and fooleries."

WAIT ON THE LORD

Yes, the things of God are always worth the wait. This truth encourages me to walk as Jesus walked. It encourages me to adopt His pace to slow down and develop the deep and meaningful relationships I was designed for. The slow pace is the only pace in which to live alongside people labeled with disabilities or to build a home alongside those in foster care. I acknowledge that the things of God are worth the wait when I don't try to rush or fix God's timing. When I remove the waste and focus on God's heart as an essential for my own.

When I do not rush God, and when I adopt the slow pace of my savior, I am better able to learn the lessons He has in store for me. This is true when the teacher has their own pace. When I slow down, I can wait on God's timing. I can have the rest the Psalmist speaks of. I see that when the Lord is my shepherd, I will have no wants, I will rest, I will be satiated, and I will be protected. Waiting on the Lord is not like waiting on a bus or train. Rather, it is the rest that comes from trust. It is a trust that comes from keeping God in the forefront of our being. Brother Lawrence recognized that God "does not ask much of us," he continued that as we keep God in mind, as we trust and rest, we "need not cry out very loudly" when we are in distress, for God "is nearer to us than we think."

Again, we see the Psalmist speak to this truth when he declares "I remain confident of this: I will see the goodness of the Lord in the land of the living. Wait for the Lord; be strong and take heart and wait for the Lord." (Psalm 27:13-14, NIV) This is a Psalm of trust. God's timing is better than ours. Wait. Trust. Wait and Trust. As I wait, I also trust. As I wait and trust, I look to see the story God writes unfold in ways that I could not have imagined. I see the story unfold in ways that do not coincide with my timing. In ways that cannot be rushed, in ways only God can unfold.

Through foster care and adoption, through cancer and recovery, through autism and disability, I have had to learn to wait and trust. In the over twelve years since I first met my incredibly amazing daughter, there have been, to use Summer's words, "sad parts," there have been disappointments, there have been frustrations and tears. Yet, this amazing individual has always, always, again I say, always shown me the truth that the things of God are ALWAYS worth the wait.

Conclusion

While we begin our stories like coins, sheep, and prodigal children. In short, we begin our stories lost. This loss, however, is not the end of the story. So, while we wait for God to write the story. While we wait for God to generously pour out in buckets and buckets all the great things He has in store, I learn that waiting for God to bring about His story is always, always, always worth it.

In the Fall of 2014 as Summer entered third grade, an amazing story unfolded. Summer was placed in a segregated classroom for most of her day, yet she enjoyed recess and lunchtime with the rest of the third graders. One afternoon while hanging out in her usual spot near the slide, she met another third grader named Jennifer. Jennifer was a popular kid. Jennifer was smart and heavily involved in school and community activities. Summer and Jennifer immediately connected. They became friends. Jennifer was not assigned to be a "buddy" or a "mentor." Rather, they were simply friends. Year in and year out, the two remained friends, even into middle school.

They were not each other's only friends. Jennifer, as I mentioned, was very popular. Yet, she always made time for Summer. As a parent of a child labeled with disabilities, it is often too common to see only paid, or assigned, "friends" in our daughter's life. So, to see a young woman openly welcome our daughter into her life was significant. Yet, as you can imagine, being a popular tween who chose to hang out with a socially awkward girl in special education presented certain challenges.

Jennifer's mother, Rosa, loved Summer and welcomed her as well. Rosa shared the following story with Mandy:

Jennifer came home one day from school and told her mom about her day. She told her mom that some of her friends did not like her hanging out with "one of those kids." In fact, they confronted her and asked in a disgusted, but questioning tone. "Why do you hang out with Summer?"

"What did you tell them?" Rosa asked.

Jennifer said, "I told them that Summer is my friend, and walked away."

Rosa was proud of her daughter, but she had her own question. "Jennifer," Rosa asked "why are you and Summer friends?"

Jennifer responded, "All of my other friends always want me to be a certain way, to do certain things, or act a certain way. But Summer lets me be myself. She doesn't put demands on me, and I don't put demands on her."

I remember the day Mandy listened to Rosa share that story. I remember watching her tear up as the realization that Jennifer had just spoken to the dreams of so many parents of children labeled with disabilities. While professionals love to wax on about goals and objectives, for many parents and caregivers we desperately want to see someone love and accept our child who isn't required to do so. So, it was a blessing when Jennifer described genuine friendship. She highlighted the fact that relationships, real quality relationships, require opportunity. They value presence over accomplishment. Genuine friendships reject demands, ambition, and conformity and, instead, value presence, authenticity, and time.

So here was a girl who as early as ten years of age, could break through fear and offer relationship to someone desperately in need, but also grateful for it. Jennifer is a bright example of how things can be. She is also a reminder that while Summer continues to teach important lessons, there are others who have so much wisdom and knowledge to offer. These "teachers" are often not where we expect to find them. They are often missing pulpits, advanced degrees, or social standing. Maybe that is the most important lesson. Maybe we need to tear down our prejudice and expectations to look beyond our bias so that we might receive the lessons God has in store. Even from the most surprising of places.

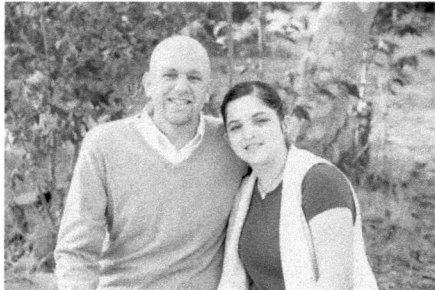

Summer and her daddy. Life is good.

Acknowledgements

This book would not be possible without the insight, wisdom, and indomitable spirit of Summer Joy Hoggatt. I appreciate you and am thankful for the lessons you teach me, beyond this project. I love being in your family. I am incredibly proud of the way you share your story and allow me to share your story as well. I pray that I have done your story justice.

The lessons and ideas in this book came from the life and heart of Summer Joy. However, putting words to those ideas came through meaningful discussions with people whom I trust and greatly appreciate. Mandy listened to me think through these ideas late at night and gifted me her time and support. Friends and family have listened to my ideas and shared their own hearts which has furthered my perspective in ways I cannot begin to show nmy appreciation for.

Prior to the writing of this text my ideas, as well as my understanding of my own daughter's wisdom has been shaped by the love, hospitality, and friendship poured into our lives by too many amazing people to name. However, please know that you are appreciated and loved.

Finally, I am thankful that you have taken the time to read and share in our story. We hope that you are encouraged by what you find.

About the Author

Mike is the President of the Disability Ministry Conference, and organization whose mission is to "Advance Quality Disability Ministry by Coming Together to Learn, Connect & Collaborate."

Summer, Mike, Elijah, and Mandy Hoggatt

He holds Masters in both Special Education and Public Policy as well a Ph.D. in Higher Education Policy with an emphasis in Disability Policy. His work on disability policy as well as the intersection of faith and disabilities has been published in various outlets including The Journal of the Christian Institute on Disability, The Community College Review, The Community College Journal of Research and Practice, PRISM Magazine, and Focus on the Family.

Dr. Hoggatt has served on the board of directors for Friendship Ministries, Inc., an international ministry whose purpose is to provide resources that support faith formation and congregational inclusion with individuals with intellectual disability. Mike regularly consults and provides training to families, disability ministries, faith-communities, and related non-profit organizations. If you would like to book Mike for a training or speaking event contact him @ www.hoggattconsulting.com

Lightning Source UK Ltd.
Milton Keynes UK
UKHW020630081220
374827UK00013B/1058